516.9.52

THE
MOSLEM
WORLD

Countries where Islam prevails

*Countries with a minor
proportion of Moslems*

ARAL
SEA

L. BALKHASH

A   S   I   A

TURKESTAN

PEKING

ERAT   KABUL   PESHAWAR

AFGHANISTAN   KHYBER
PASS

Hoang-ho

CHINA

LAHORE
PUNJAB
DELHI   ALIGARH

Indus

Brahmaputra

Yang-tse-Kiang

Ganges   ASSAM

BENGAL

INDIA

HYDERABAD

SIAM

MALAY
STATES

SUMATRA

BORNEO

MALAYSIA

JAVA

I N D I A N

O C E A N

AUSTRALIA

A.F.H.

I. Kemp.

W. Clandon.

Photo   "*The Times*," 22nd Jan. 1925

THE ARABS' NEW HIGHWAYS

The Damascus-to-Baghdad motor service (p. 12) meets an aeroplane of the Baghdad-to-Cairo "mail" in difficulties.
The wireless aerial mast was rigged in the desert to call help from Baghdad.

THE MOSLEM WORLD
IN REVOLUTION

BY

W. WILSON CASH
D.S.O., O.B.E.
*Formerly Assistant Principal Chaplain
to the Egyptian Expeditionary Force*

LONDON
EDINBURGH HOUSE PRESS
2 EATON GATE, S.W.1
1926

Published by the

EDINBURGH HOUSE PRESS

2 Eaton Gate, Sloane Square, S.W.1

*A detailed list of publications will be
sent on application*

First Edition, March 1925
Second Edition, June 1925
Third Edition, July 1925
Fourth Edition, November 1925
Fifth Edition, February 1926

*Printed in Scotland
by Turnbull & Spears, Edinburgh*

TO
MY BELOVED
COMPANION AND FELLOW-WORKER
IN THE GOSPEL, MY WIFE
THIS BOOK IS
DEDICATED

FOREWORD

BY THE

BISHOP OF EGYPT AND THE SUDAN

THE author of this book is one of the few men able from practical experience in the Moslem World to write on this subject. For many years he has worked in the Delta in Egypt, where the population is almost entirely Moslem. He is an expert in Islamics—can both read and speak the Arabic language—and has the gift, unusual in an Englishman, of holding the attention of an Arab-speaking crowd by his preaching.

During the war he became Assistant Principal Chaplain to the Egyptian Expeditionary Force, in which he served with distinction, and, as a student of Islam, had an excellent opportunity of seeing the effect of the war on the Moslem population. Since the war his duties have taken him all over the Near East and brought him in touch with Moslems of the Sudan, Egypt, and Palestine. At Omdurman the Moslem notables gave him a good reception, and invited him to speak to them on religion—when by his breadth of outlook and fair speech, he won their friendship. He is always fair to Islam, whose good points as well as inherent weaknesses he recognizes fully. Both the author of the book and the writer of this Foreword are proud to reckon amongst their friends Moslems who talk most naturally with them about their religion.

There are some who shake their heads in despondency at recent happenings, such as the divisions in Islam during the war, the fall of the Caliphate, and the expulsion from Mecca of its rightful heir. This volume describes vividly and accurately the process of revolution now taking place. It expresses the opinion that the moment has come when the Christian Church, in the spirit of her Master, can, without contention, offer her vital force that those who live in Moslem lands may break the fetters which hold them back from their right to keep abreast of the great civilizing powers in the world.

LLEWELLYN H. GWYNNE

KHARTOUM
February 1925

4

AUTHOR'S PREFACE

As this book goes to press news comes through from North Africa of the capture of Rasuli, the Spanish ally, by Abd el Krim, leader of the rebel Arab force. The Spaniards have come up against the old Arab fighting spirit, and have had to evacuate one position after another until they are now fighting with their backs to the sea and in danger of being driven out of North Africa. This is the second time since the Great War that a European power has been defeated by a Moslem army, for it is less than three years since Mustapha Kemal drove Greece out of Asia Minor and defied the might of Europe. Within the last few months the Wahabis of Arabia have attacked and occupied Mecca and compelled King Hussein to abdicate. The expulsion of the Caliph from Constantinople in 1922 created a ferment from India to North Africa, and changes since then have been so rapid it is difficult to say what the outcome will be. "Revolution" does not seem therefore any too strong a word to apply to the Moslem world to-day.

The remarkable thing in the present situation is the changed attitude of the people towards life itself. As the following pages try to show, Moslem minds are opening to new ideas and impressions. Moslems are reading more widely and are studying the science of the West. Many are no longer content with the old Koranic laws in regard to women, and insist on education for both boys and girls. Out of this ferment, change, and revolution, nations are literally leaping into new life.

Prior to these changes, missionaries, though few in number, were established in many strategic centres in Islam, and through revolution, war, and turmoil they have carried on their work quietly and persistently. Social work through hospitals and dispensaries has given the people new ideals in many Moslem lands; in fact missionary methods have been copied by Moslems, until to-day we find Moslem societies running free dispensaries, hospitals and orphanages. Similarly, in many cases the missionaries have been the pioneers in education. Missionary efforts have thus been fruitful in many directions, the result of which is best seen perhaps in the attitude of Moslems to-day to missionaries and their message. Converts from Islam to Christianity are increasing, and through revolutions that are shaking the nations there emerges a great quest for *something*—something which followers of the Christian Faith believe they hold in the Gospel of Jesus Christ.

This little book has been written to show how the great changes in the Islamic world are affecting the life of the people, and to bring home to our Churches the urgent need for advance in missionary enterprise amongst Moslems in this day of opportunity.

I wish to express my gratitude to the many missionaries in the Moslem world who have so kindly supplied me with information from their fields.

W. WILSON CASH

LONDON
February 1925

CONTENTS

ILLUSTRATIONS

THE MOSLEM WORLD
IN REVOLUTION

CHAPTER I

THE STORY OF ISLAM

WE arrived at Damascus railway station one morning in 1913 to say good-bye to some of the pilgrims who were starting down the Mecca railway. At the booking-office we were reminded by a kindly clerk that beyond a certain point no Christian could travel, no ticket could be issued to him, and were he to venture into this closed area death would be the penalty. Islam [1] had made so sacred the land around the birthplace of Mohammed that no Christian ought to defile it by his presence. One was reminded of the stone slabs placed in the outer court of the Jewish Temple at Jerusalem, beyond which Gentiles were forbidden to go under penalty of death. Our first impression that morning was of the exclusiveness of Islam.

As we waited for the train to start we jostled with a motley crowd of pilgrims from India, Syria, Palestine,

[1] An Arabic word for "resignation to the will of God"—used by Mohammedans for their religion. Those who profess the religion of Islam are called Moslems (also spelt Muslims) or Mohammedans. "Moslem" is from the same root verb as "Islam," and means a surrendered one, or one who has received Islam.

Turkey, Europe, and parts of Northern Africa. They differed widely in garb and language, but were united in one burning faith and passionate desire to perform the pilgrimage and visit the tomb of the Prophet, thus storing up merit that would ensure eternal life after death. It gave one the impression of the solidarity of Islam through its oneness of interest, the common brotherhood, the unity of a faith that held the loyalty of people as widely separated as those of Turkestan and Morocco, and India and Palestine. The one thing in common was faith in God and trust in His Prophet.

We began to mix with the throng of pilgrims ; some we could talk to, and we asked them who they were. We received one invariable answer—" Musilmeen " (Moslems). It was only after two or three questions that they guessed that we wanted to know their country. Nationality seemed eclipsed and left behind in a wider movement, the race question forgotten in something that transcended their own lands and customs. They were " Moslems," and their religion towered above all that was personal, national, and local in an international unity that meant to them the triumph of God and His Prophet throughout the world.

As we walked away from the station that morning we turned over in our minds the impressions we had felt. Here was a faith, virile and strong, self-propagating and extending ; a faith holding sway over two hundred and thirty million people; a faith for which men were prepared to fight, sacrifice, and suffer; a faith that had swept away caste and to a large extent class distinction, and that stood for a common brotherhood within the " House of Islam."

Damascus again, October 1918. There were converging from East and West on this, the oldest city in the world, two allied armies—one a British, the other an Arab force. The town was in the hands of a third army, a Turkish force, composed of soldiers recruited from Palestine, Syria, Mesopotamia, as well as Turkey. Mohammedans were thus fighting Mohammedans, and East was mingled with West in a confused mixture of races. The British and Arab armies occupied the city—once the centre of a great Moslem power. British soldiers safeguarded the lives of civilians, and Arab cavalry swept through the streets, driving the Turks before them north towards Constantinople. An historic occasion it was when King Feisul, the leader of the Arab army —now [1] the ruler of Mesopotamia—met Lord Allenby in Damascus. It was East greeting West, Mohammedan shaking hands with Christian ; it was the beginning of a day when Islam as a world-unit would cease to be, and when national claims would take precedence of the old theory of Islam as a Church-State knowing no geographical boundaries.

The year 1923 found us once more in Damascus. As we walked through the streets, a few pilgrims were to be seen here and there gathering for their long journey to Mecca. But as we passed through the bazaars we saw changes everywhere : a new spirit of independence and liberty was a prominent feature;

[1] February 1925.

the day of the Turk had gone ; European banks were open again, and shops were stocked with goods from Manchester. What attracted our attention most of all was a small convoy of American motor-cars drawn up by the side of the road. A crowd had gathered round with obvious interest, and we drew near to find out the destination of these cars. The driver of one of them—a lean wiry American—standing by his car, said, " We start to-day for Baghdad ; this is the motor mail service, and we now run a regular weekly service of cars from Damascus to Baghdad." And he added, " Only last week we performed the journey in nineteen hours, a record for us." Our minds went back to our journey through Syria to Damascus ten years before. Then not a motor-car was to be seen, Turkish misrule seemed in evidence everywhere: Islam was all-powerful.

Moving through the crowd this time one seemed to breathe a new atmosphere, and the impression we gained was that the Arabs were now thinking more in terms of Arab nationality than of Islamic unity. We saw these wild sons of the desert caught in a stream of world renaissance, determined at last, after centuries of Turkish oppression, to live their own lives and to be free and independent. There were evident signs of a clash of race between the Arabs and the French, who at present hold the mandate for Syria. A new sense of their racial and national importance had come to the people, and they moved through the streets no longer with an air of sub-jection, but with pride and confidence in their race and country.

Damascus to-day is a railway centre; motor roads are radiating from it in all directions. The Bible Society agent only a few months ago was able with a small motor-car to cross the desert, visit such places as Palmyra and towns on the Euphrates, and travel thousands of miles, distributing Bibles wherever he went. The East is changing, and changing so rapidly that we stand in some bewilderment and watch the march of a liberated people towards their destiny.

．　　．　　．　　．　　．　　．

The Founder of Islam

Mohammed, "the Prophet of Arabia," was born in Mecca in A.D. 570. At an early age he was left an orphan and was adopted by an uncle, who later in life stood as Mohammed's protector against the fury of pagan Mecca. From a shepherd boy he grew to be a camel-driver. At the age of twenty-five he married a wealthy lady, Khadija, and settled down to a quiet domestic life in Mecca. There were no signs in Mohammed's early years of any great hidden forces in his character. The religious influences in his life were probably mainly Jewish, for his wife was a member of a small sect in Arabia trying to proclaim a new faith in the one God. Mohammed was shocked by the superstitions and the paganism of his time, and was an easy convert to the creed of his wife. But at the age of forty he carried his creed a step further. He began not simply to speak of God as One, but spent days and months in trying to realize in his life the reality of God. He spent days in a cave in meditation, and here he believed that God had called him to be the last of the great Prophets to lead the world back to the one true faith. After this he developed a theology—a belief in a future life, a heaven and a hell, a doctrine of angels, jinn, and demons—and he began in secret to teach his new faith. As converts joined the ranks, Mohammed became bolder and preached more openly. Trouble followed, and he was driven out of Mecca and fled for safety to Medina—a town about ten days' camel journey north of Mecca. This was the great turning-point in Mohammed's life. Had the Arabs in Mecca treated him with a little more tolerance there would probably have been no religion of Islam to-day. Tribal warfare broke out, and the Battle of Badr decided the fate of Arabia, when Mohammed with a small army of three hundred men defeated the Meccans a thousand strong. From this time until his death in 632, we have an amazing picture of this shepherd boy grown into an Arab of the Arabs and uniting the warring tribes of Arabia under one rule.

While Mohammed was calling the tribes of Arabia to challenge the world and giving to his soldiers a new battle-cry of the sword of Mohammed, a small band of missionaries had landed in England under the leadership of St Augustine. Arabia and England were both wrapped in pagan superstition : a messenger of the Cross was seeking to win England for Christ, while Mohammed was cementing Arabia in a new faith. Neither knew of the other's work, but, ever since, Islam and Christianity have been facing each other, both claiming to hold a divine message, both missionary in outlook, the one proclaiming the sword of " God and Mohammed," the other teaching the way of the Prince of Peace.

Before Mohammed died he saw the most distant parts of his land accepting him as God's heaven-sent Prophet. He recaptured Mecca, cleansed the Kaaba —the sacred shrine of paganism—from its idols, and converted it into a mosque—a Mohammedan place of worship. He sent messengers east and west to proclaim his divine mission and to summon the rulers of the world to obedience to his faith. Then he gathered a small army of three thousand young men, who encamped outside Medina, with the object of sending them to fight the Roman Empire.

It was while this army was in preparation for a war of Islam outside Arabia that Mohammed died. The army and the people were beside themselves with grief. The women wailed, shrieked, and covered their heads with mud and dirt ; the men declared that their Prophet could not be dead. All business in Medina was suspended, the army was forbidden to leave, and the town completely lost its head. Then Abu Bakr, one of the finest men Arabia ever produced, stood up in front of the people, and with calm dignity in the midst of grief and turmoil, declared: " Mohammed is dead: the Faith lives." He was at once acclaimed the Caliph, or successor of the Prophet, and after the burial and mourning ceremonies were over, he, with dauntless faith, ordered the little army to march out and invade Syria. The mantle of Mohammed seemed to have fallen upon him, for he looked out upon the world, east and

west, with a great ideal of world conquest and world
dominion for God and His Prophet.

The First Hundred Years

At that time Constantinople was the capital of the
Roman Empire, and had for some centuries been
decaying. Of the countries of the East, Persia was
the most powerful. And the armies of these two
rival races and civilizations were constantly at war.
Roman troops rolled forward in mass formation to
Mesopotamia only to be driven back again and again
beyond the Taurus Mountains by a Persian force.
Shortly before the rise of Islam, East and West had
been involved in a noisy conflict and the respective
armies had rocked backwards and forwards; with the
result that when the Arabs set out to attack them
both Rome and Persia were weakened and unprepared
for the onslaught. The accumulated wealth of centuries lay in the Eastern and Western capitals as
though only waiting to become the plunder of these
warriors of the desert.

It was at this point that two Moslem armies set out
from Arabia, one east and one west. They attacked
at the same time Syria and Persia and were everywhere victorious. They offered the inhabitants of
each city they conquered the choice of three things :
to pay tribute, become Moslem, or die. The plunder
was so enormous that every soldier became rich, and
new armies were rapidly raised from the converts to
Islam in the conquered territories. A well-trained
and powerful Roman army was crushed to pieces at
the river Yarmuk in Transjordania. The river was

choked with Roman dead, and the Emperor abandoned Syria to the Arabs. Damascus fell, Antioch was captured, Jerusalem surrendered to Omar, the second Caliph. All Palestine and Syria came under Moslem sway, an army swept down on Egypt, and in a brief campaign the country was overrun by Arab hordes. Meanwhile the army fighting eastwards through Mesopotamia met the might of Persia in a three days' battle; the Persian army was utterly defeated, and its leader was found dead on the battle-field at the end of the fight. The armies in the East then swept north through Turkestan towards India and China.

At this stage a curious and for Europe a merciful turn was taken in the Moslem advance. The armies in the West turned along the North African coast and swept, wave after wave, right up by the Strait of Gibraltar. Had they concentrated their efforts on Constantinople, occupied the Taurus Mountains and the country beyond, there is little doubt that their attacks would have carried them into the very heart of Europe before the end of the eighth century. As it was the Arabs came into Europe via Africa and Spain to meet in France a determined Christian force under Charles Martel, which checked the spread of Islam westwards at the Pyrenees in A.D. 732.

Gibbon thus sums up this first spread of Mohammedan power : " In the ten years of the administration of Omar the Saracens reduced to obedience 36,000 cities and castles, destroyed 4000 temples and churches of the non-believers, and erected 1400 mosques for the exercise of the religion of Mohammed."

B

One hundred years after Mohammed settled in Medina his followers occupied territory stretching from India to the Atlantic. Gibraltar, a proud possession of the British Empire to-day, takes its name from this period. It is a combination of two Arabic words, Gabel (mountain) and Tarik (the name of the Arab leader).

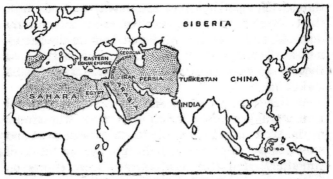

Extent of Islam, A.D. 800

By the middle of the eighth century the Moslem attack on the world had come to an end and the clan spirit of the Arabs divided Islam and reduced its fighting strength. The Mohammedan world was distracted by civil war and split in two, and never again were the Arabs able to impose their rule and religion on the world in the same way. Dissension led to a decline in Mohammedan faith and practice, and with increase of wealth the Moslems forgot the precepts of their Prophet. Some openly mocked at the sacred book of Islam—the Koran—and broke the rules about eating pork and drinking wine. Luxury killed the puritan spirit in Islam, and the people imitated the vices of the West without learning anything of the moral force of the Christian faith.

Mohammedan conquests had brought the Arabs into contact with Greek thought, Eastern Christianity, the science and learning of the West, and the mysticism of the East. The Arab is a man of little imagination and originality, but he is a good copyist, and contact with non-Moslem thought and life led to an awakening in the Arab world. Universities were established for the study of the Koran and the Arabic language. To these subjects were added mathematics, medicine, and other sciences. While these movements were influencing for all time the life of the East, missionaries of the Christian Church were travelling through Europe in a great evangelistic campaign for the conversion of our pagan forefathers to the Gospel.

The East was at that time undoubtedly ahead of Europe, both in regard to learning and social life. The two greatest figures in history at this period were Charlemagne in the West and Haroun al-Raschid in the East ; they divided between them the greater portion of the then known world. They never met, and yet they corresponded with each other. Haroun is the Arabic word for Aaron. In the eighth century he was the Caliph of Islam and ruled an Eastern Empire with Baghdad as his capital. He is the hero of many of the stories in the *Arabian Nights*, and is renowned for his display of old Arab chivalry, hospitality, and courtesy. Owing to the conquest of Jerusalem by the Arabs, Haroun had in his possession the keys of the Church of the Holy Sepulchre at

Jerusalem. These he despatched to Charlemagne, the representative of Christianity in the West, an act that was meant to seal a new friendship between East and West, Islam and Christianity.

Turkey comes to the Fore

While the Norman power was developing in Europe a new force was arising in the East—the Mongol hosts of Central Asia, which swept westward right across Asia to Russia in 1255. Raymond Lull, who was living at that time, saw the Mongol armies advancing into Europe, and he paid a special visit to the Pope to plead for an effective missionary force for their conversion. He saw the open door, the Church's opportunity, and the great possibilities for good or evil in this Mongol conquest. With prophetic instinct he saw too the catastrophe it would be to the Church and to Europe if these newcomers came under the sway of Islam. But the Christian Church seemed to be in a hopeless state of moral and intellectual decay, without faith or energy, and the God-given opportunity was lost. The Mongols in China and Central Asia turned to Buddhism, and in Turkestan and South Russia they embraced Islam.

A little band of fugitives from Turkestan fled before the Mongol armies. They moved with their herds westward, and in course of time established themselves in Asia Minor as far as the Bosphorus. These " Turks " founded the Ottoman or Turkish Empire, and in 1453 attacked and captured Constantinople. The Roman Emperor was killed, the city looted, and many of the people massacred. The great Church of Santa Sophia, which Justinian the Great had built in 532, was plundered of its treasure and turned into a mosque. This event sent a wave of excitement throughout Europe, the results of which were to be felt for many days to come.

Extent of Islam, A.D. 1480

Throughout the century following the capture of Constantinople the Turkish pressure upon Europe was heavy and continuous. The trade routes to the East, which hitherto had been via the Mediterranean, were interrupted, and Europe became an isolated continent. Shut in by the vast Atlantic Ocean on the west and by a Mohammedan force in Eastern Europe and on all points around the Mediterranean Sea, she found her markets in the East closed. Trade was rapidly coming to a standstill, and new outlets had to be found.

The Decline of Turkey

In 1492 Columbus set out westward to discover, as he believed, a new route to India. In 1498, the year when Columbus first set foot on the mainland of North America, Vasco da Gama found the route to India round the Cape of Good Hope. These and kindred adventures led to an expansion of European ideas. The developments of science, the exploration of the world, the great dissemination of knowledge through printing, and the spread of a new impulse for freedom and liberty—all led to the check of Moslem aggression, and for the next four hundred years the world was dominated by the increasing power of European nations.

Turkey made her last attack on Vienna in 1683 and failed. From the seventeenth century to the present day Moslem history is one long story of losses. All North Africa was taken from Turkey by Europe. The Balkan States one by one gained their independence. Turkey did not march with the times ; in policy and thought she was unprogressive and out of sympathy with everything non-Moslem. Arabia fell back into its old tribal state, and all semblance of unity disappeared. Egypt and the Sudan were occupied by Great Britain. India passed entirely out of Moslem control and became a British possession. Turkey was referred to in European Courts as " the sick man," and politicians discussed what they should do with this land when the sick man came to die—and then they were faced, not with the collapse of Turkey, but with the Great War of 1914.

CHAPTER II

NEW INFLUENCES IN THE MOSLEM WORLD

THE Arab was disturbed by rumours. Wonderful tales were afloat from Damascus down to the sacred cities of Mecca and Medina. The camel drivers scoffed and the traders shook their heads. What was agitating their minds? The story of an "iron road" to be built from Damascus to Medina, an impossible story, it seemed to the sons of the desert, of a steam engine that could pull great wagons full of goods along iron rails. The beginning of the famous pilgrim railway did not dispel doubt. The owners of camels asked incredulously whether a train could carry as much as a camel? Slowly the line grew, and when the first train ran into Medina railway station, Arabs crowded in from the desert to see this new wonder. Some, who had only heard the stories, were still doubtful as to the truth of this wonderful invention, when to their amazement there poured from the train scores of people, boxes, and luggage of all descriptions, and, like the Queen of Sheba, there was no more spirit in them. Their one exclamation was, " O wonder of God!" In the West, familiar as we are with our railway system, it is difficult for us to imagine the revolution involved in this narrow-gauge line to Medina. The Arabs felt nothing could be the same again. The old Arab world of seclusion had gone for ever, and the holy places of Islam were linked by a modern invention to the West. The camel drivers were the first to wake up to the meaning of it all. They said, " Our trade is gone. No one will now want camels," and they promptly tore up a large section of the line. But the railway had come to stay, and the Arabs, after doubting, demurring and complaining, came to adopt the railway as their own and to use it.

This event, which marked the opening of the twentieth century, will illustrate the changes that were then coming to the House of Islam.

The Moslem world by 1900 was largely under the control of European powers, and the purely Islamic countries were either so shrunken in size, or so backward and undeveloped, that they had ceased to count in the councils of the nations. European statesmen described Islam as a dying faith, and they predicted its eclipse by modern Western civilization. Politically and socially decay had set in, and the question openly discussed was whether Islam could be revived and reformed.

Contact with the West was bringing about great changes, especially to the educated classes, in outlook, habit, and thought. Europeanized Egyptians, for example, lost their respect for the religious teachers of Islam, and regarded them as social derelicts who had to be tolerated for political purposes, and even to be made use of for propaganda when the masses had to be roused. The reason for this was that there are, in most Moslem countries, two distinct and contradictory types of education. One is the old system based on the Koran. In such institutions as the Azhar University of Cairo the Koran is the basis of all teaching. The students memorize the book from cover to cover—it is about the size of our New Testament. Many of them learn to repeat it without a mistake, and they have been known to rattle off the whole of it in nine hours. The Koran teaches that the world is flat, and one verse says Alexander the Great travelled so far west that he came to the place where the sun sets, and " behold it sets in a pool of mud " ! While this form of education is being given within the sacred precincts of mosques, only a short distance away the sons of the very men studying and teaching the Koran are being educated on Western lines by young men from English universities. The camel and the train are again in opposition. The ancient and the modern types of education meet, not in any school or college, but in the homes, when the boys return for their holidays. The old men shake their heads, and the young men openly scoff at the ignorance of their parents.

The Pan-Islamic Movement

Western influence not only meant the weakening of Islamic power politically, but it also led to a widespread increase of infidelity and atheism. The leaders of religion were profoundly disturbed. They still dreamed of world power and the triumph of their religion over all others, and a new effort was made to revive Islam and to draw together Moslems everywhere in one common brotherhood. This effort was called the Pan-Islamic Movement. " It was a union of Moslems to defy and resist Christian powers and to undertake the regeneration of Islam upon Islamic lines." Its ideals were those of Abu Bakr when he set out to conquer the world in the seventh century. It was to be a League of Moslem Nations for the defence of Mohammedan power and for aggressive attempts to increase it. In the ordinary language of the day it meant the extension of Turkish rule over all Moslems.

The Sultan of Turkey was Sultan of a small empire, but he claimed to be Caliph [1] of two hundred and thirty million people, and in theory they owed him loyalty. All the powers of Europe watched the Pan-Islamic Movement with intense interest. Britain could not shut her eyes to its possibilities, for there are seventy million Moslems in India alone, and France was nervous about her North African possessions. Germany deliberately aimed at making use of the movement for her own political ends. In 1909 an envoy arrived at Peking from the Sultan of Turkey to ask for the recognition of Mohammedan consuls in China to look after Moslem interests. Here was a far-reaching move in the game. There are about nine million Moslems in China—all Chinese subjects —and the Sultan claimed, as Caliph, the right to

---

[1] The civil and religious head of the Moslem world (see p. 43). Turkish Sultans claimed the right to be Caliphs, although not Arabs, on the following grounds—the right of the sword, election, the guardianship of the two shrines (Mecca and Medina), and possession of the sacred relics.

" watch their interests." The Sultan's request was refused, and China rubbed her eyes with amazement when a few months later the German Minister at Peking informed the Chinese government that Germany had been requested by Turkey to undertake the protection of Turkish subjects in China ! Events in other directions were moving rapidly. The Balkan War stripped Turkey of most of her European territory. Italy in 1913 suddenly declared war on the Turks and annexed Tripoli.

Down to 1914 it cannot be said that the Pan-Islamic Movement had done anything practical to strengthen Islam. Politically Islam had lost rather than gained ground in the twenty - five years before the war in 1914, and the combined efforts of the religious leaders had utterly failed to check the spread of Western influence. Young men in large numbers were entering the schools and colleges, and almost all the old conservative families who could afford it were sending their sons to schools of the Western type. The younger generation of educated people were poles apart from their parents in social, religious and political thought. Territory had been lost and reform efforts had made little headway, and when Turkey entered the War in November 1914 on the side of Germany, it remained to be seen what hold the Caliph had upon Islam as a whole.

Now it should be remembered that in the Moslem world there is a wide difference between a " war " and a " holy war." The Crimean War in 1854, for instance, involved Turkey, but it was not a " holy war." A holy war to Moslems is a religious war

with those who are unbelievers.   It is laid down in
the Koran as a religious duty, established by divine
authority and ordered by God for the purpose of
increasing Islam in the world.   One verse in the
Koran says : " The fires of hell shall not touch the
legs of him who shall be covered with the dust of
battle in the road of God."

The question that Moslems from Africa to India
had to face in 1914 was whether the conflict of Europe
should be regarded as a "holy war."   Turkey knew
the value of such a battle-cry, and in Constantinople
there was a thrilling scene when the Sultan, as Caliph
of Islam, declared a *holy* war against the allied armies.
Intense enthusiasm was aroused by the unfurling of
a special green flag which definitely marked the war
as religious, and Moslems the world over were called
upon to fight in the defence of Islam.   The people of
India, Egypt, and Arabia, asked, "Are we to fight for
our faith or for Germany ? "   The Minister of War
in Turkey made impassioned speeches and declared
that the War was Turkey's great opportunity to win
back to Islam its lost position in the world.   The
appeal fell flat.   Moslems who lived under the British
flag knew their Faith was in no danger.   They had
seen many years of liberty of conscience, and they
refused to be led by Turkey ; the religious leaders in
Africa and India pronounced the war to be non-
religious and not a " holy war " at all.

The most significant answer to Turkey's appeal
came, however, when the Sherif of Mecca, the
Guardian of the Holy Places, threw off all allegiance
to Turkey, joined the Allies, and fought on their

side against his co-religionists, the Turks. The reason was that the old feud between Turk and Arab had never died out. The Arabs hated the Turks, and the Turks, in turn, despised the Arabs; consequently an Arab did not look upon the War simply as a Western affair. Germany against the Allies was a side show to them. They fought for Arab independence against their ancient enemies.

Moslems at the Peace Conference

When the War ended, many parts of the Moslem world were represented at the Peace Conference. Mohammedan leaders, the war Allies of the Entente Powers, sat in Paris with European statesmen to discuss the terms of peace as they affected Moslem lands.

Paris in 1919 seemed scarcely recognizable as the capital of France. It became a vast cosmopolitan centre, teeming with strange and curiously dressed peoples. In the streets were heard the languages of races and tribes of four continents. There were guests of France from far-off Turkestan and Persia; Armenians were present to represent to Europe the sorrows of a stricken race; sons of the Arabian desert stalked proudly through the streets on their way to the Conference to demand from the Turks their independence and freedom, won by plucky fights on many a battle-field; there were men with patriarchal beards, and young rulers of Indian States. The yellows, the browns, the blacks, and the whites, all mingled freely together, and for a time it seemed as though Paris might solve the clash of colour. Moslem leaders were brought into the inner councils of Europe at last—and what was their purpose ? Not to defend the old Pan-Islamic scheme, for some were there to demand a new liberty, of which they had been robbed for so long by the Caliph of Constantinople, others to defend the rights of their nation. All had caught the magic word "self-determination," and nationality seemed a bigger issue than Islam.

When treaties were signed it was found that the Turkish Empire had shrunk still further in the process of making peace : Syria, Palestine, Arabia, and Mesopotamia to the borders of Persia had all gone. British and French flags were seen where the Crescent,[1] the symbol of Turkish power, had proudly flown for centuries before. A Moslem writer, Sheikh Mohammed Shakir, in an article in a Cairo daily paper, summing up what the War meant to Islam, wrote :—

Do Moslems forget that they lost in the Great War the whole heritage of the first century of Islam, those lands which have proclaimed the greatness of Islam in its early victories for the last thirteen centuries ? We have not forgotten, nor shall we let Islam forget, that in the War was lost the first capital of Islam, dating from the time when the Umayyid dynasty was founded in Damascus. We have not forgotten, nor shall we permit the Moslem world to forget, that in the War was lost the second capital of Islam, dating from the time when the Abbaside dynasty was founded in Baghdad. We have not forgotten, nor shall we

[1] A representation of the half moon. It was the emblem of the Greek before it became that of Turkish rule, but it was not adopted by the Turks from the Greeks. It had been used hundreds of years before in Central Asia by the Tartars

allow the Moslem world to forget, that in the War was lost the Holy City [Jerusalem] and the far distant mosque for whose purity [from infidels] and reservation in holiness Islam has shed her most precious blood and the lives of her heroes from the outset of Islam to the days of the victorious Saladin [in the Crusades]. And we have not forgotten, nor shall we allow the Moslem world to forget, that in the War there was lost the security of Mecca and Medina, the two venerated spots in one of which is the Kaaba and in the other the dust of the chosen of God.

Baghdad (once the capital of Haroun al-Raschid), Damascus (the oldest city in the world, and a former centre of Moslem power), Jerusalem (famous among Moslems for the Crusades), Mecca and Medina (the most sacred spots in all Islam)—all lost, says this writer. These cities are all historic names in the world of Islam. They represented the triumph of Moslem armies, the spread of Arab culture, the defeat of Christian forces, and they were landmarks in the spread of Mohammedanism towards world conquest.

No wonder the results of the War spread dismay in Moslem hearts. They saw France in occupation of Syria ; Great Britain in Palestine, Mesopotamia, and Egypt ; the King of the Hejaz free and independent of Turkish authority and rule. Turkey lay crushed and broken, bankrupt and defenceless. Can we imagine what this meant to Moslems ? Supposing we had lost the war, and half England were occupied by a foreign power, and Canada, New Zealand, Australia, and India, had passed out of our control ! Such a paralyzing blow would have staggered us and would

have given us a crushing feeling of despair. Yet this
is very much what happened to the Moslem world
when the Peace Treaty was signed. The Powers of
the West seemed to dominate the world. The Pan-
Islamic scheme had failed to make good, and it looked
as though the break-up of the Moslem world was
completed. It was a dark hour for Islam, but hope
was nearer at hand than was imagined.

A New Leader

At this juncture a young Turkish officer attracted
attention by his appeal for recruits and his efforts to
save what was left of Turkey. Mustapha Kemal
Pasha had rendered great service to Turkey in Galli-
poli. He had fought on the Gaza front in Palestine,
and was early marked out as a young officer of great
promise and ability, both resourceful and energetic.
The whole Moslem world centred its attention on
him. Released Turkish prisoners of war returned to
their homes in 1919 and joined the new army under
this young leader. The Powers insisted that Turkey
should put a stop to this recruiting, but the Sultan
was powerless to act. Mustapha Kemal was sum-
moned to Constantinople to be tried by court-martial,
but he refused to obey the order and increased in
strength. The Turkish government condemned him
as a rebel, but his popularity increased. When a
Greek army in 1922 attempted to take possession of
a part of Asia Minor the decisive moment arrived.
Mustapha took the field with his new force, all war
veterans. The Greeks were defeated, and Smyrna
was captured, burned, and sacked. Unspeakable

A NATIONALIST UNION FLAG

This flag, showing the Cross and the Crescent, was used by Christians and Moslems in Egypt who joined forces during the Nationalist rising of 1919 (p. 38).

Photo by THE MOSQUE AT WOKING, SURREY *F. D Walker*

" Aligarh (in India) and Woking (in England) stand for a new type of Moslem apologetic" (p. 87).

horrors followed, and a large and flourishing city was reduced to ruins. Mustapha now stood before the Moslem world as the saviour of Islam. The Sultan was deposed, and Turkey defied all Europe. The Lausanne Conference followed, and Turkey regained a strip of Europe and all Asia Minor to the borders of Syria and Mesopotamia. One Moslem writer, speaking of Mustapha at this time, says, " He rules the only independent and modern Moslem State now existing : he seems to be the only genius in the present day's world politics."

Moslems of India and Egypt found in Turkey again a new leadership. The dreams of a Pan-Islamic Power triumphing against the West seemed to be fulfilled, and Moslems were delirious with joy at the proofs of a new Islamic revival.

New Contacts through Travel and Education

We must now turn from politics to survey other recent influences on the Moslem world. The first things that struck the traveller after the War were the new facilities for travelling in lands hitherto without roads and means of transport. During the War a military railway was built from Kantara, on the Suez Canal, into Palestine. This became in peace time an entirely new railway service, with through trains from Egypt to Haifa and Jerusalem. Branch lines were developed, and to-day most of the important centres in Syria and Palestine are linked up by rail.

The mountain ranges running through the centre of Palestine make railway construction difficult and costly, and here the need was met by new motor

C

roads. Before the War scarcely a motor was to be seen in Syria and Palestine. To-day hundreds of cars are on the roads, and regular motor services run from Jerusalem in all directions. Samaria is but a two hours' journey from Jerusalem, and in a four days' tour in a car every quarter of Palestine can be visited. The Sea of Galilee, Tiberias, Nazareth, Damascus, and beyond, can all be reached by car. It would be a mistake to imagine that these cars are used only by the rich or the few. The peasants hire seats in them and travel all over the country; the fares are cheap, and a people who formerly rarely travelled more than a few miles from their homes are now visiting the most distant towns. By hiring a car in Jerusalem a tourist can travel through to Haifa in a single day. He can motor along the coast to Beirut, climb over 5000 feet on a very good road over the Lebanon mountains to Damascus, visit the Euphrates on the east and Aleppo to the north. He can cross the desert by car to Baghdad, and from there motor right across Persia. (Missionaries from Persia at the Jerusalem Conference in April 1924 came all the way by car through Mesopotamia and Damascus.) If time is pressing the traveller can fly from Amman, the capital of the new State of Transjordania, to Baghdad, by the Air Mail Service, in six hours! Imagine the influence of all this on a hitherto isolated people. Contact with people of other countries and creeds is an educational force. Old fanaticisms and prejudices wither in the light of the wider vision and outlook gained by travel.

Contrast this with the conditions of pre-war days

in Palestine. The late Dr Torrance of Tiberias had once to face a police officer who announced that the Turkish Government objected to the hymn-book he used because it contained the hymn " Hold the fort for I am coming." They said that no forts were allowed in Turkish territory. The Turks objected to the teaching of geography in a mission school in Palestine on the ground that the text-book said that the whole world did not belong to the Sultan ! A story is told in Beirut of a Turkish officer once visiting the mission printing press in that town with an order to arrest a man named Paul. When the manager of the press tried to unravel the mystery, the officer, pulling a copy of the Acts of the Apostles out of his pocket, said, " I have come to arrest the man who wrote this, ' Come over into Macedonia and help us ' " !

An elderly man in Palestine once described to me the scene in his village when his father took him to school in Jerusalem for the first time. A native carriage was hired for the journey, and as it started from the village home, relatives and friends turned out, not to bid the lad a friendly good-bye, but to chant the funeral wail and to weep over what they believed to be an evil innovation.

When Bishop Gobat went to Palestine in 1847 there was not a single school in the whole country for the natives of the land, and with great difficulty he started his first school with nine boys. In countries where the governments were Moslem before the War the education of the children was almost entirely in the hands of missionaries, and the people on the whole saw little value in schools. For ten years before the War things had slightly improved and many schools had been opened, but after the War it was found that the attitude of Moslems to education had entirely altered, and a widespread demand for learning swept through all Moslem lands. This was partly due to the fact that these countries had been facing west for five years, and partly to the new interest aroused in other lands through the demand for war news, the study of modern military inventions, and the supremacy of the West in military and scientific knowledge. Moslems had mingled freely with European troops, had fought side by side with them, and they registered a vow that when they returned to their homes they would learn more of Western nations. They would study Western books, copy their methods, and in time make the East as great and as strong as the West, and thus be able to stand up against what they called Western aggression and domination. Mission schools were flooded with applications from Moslem parents for their children to be entered as pupils. Some schools could have been filled twice over with Moslem pupils alone. The fear of Christian teaching no longer seemed to keep them back, and boys of fifteen who had not entered a school all through the War were found sitting with boys of ten eagerly learning the elementary lessons of a lower first form.

This contact with the West produced other results. Thousands of North African Moslems found employment in France. Large numbers of Moslems visited Europe to see for themselves the countries of which they had heard so much. This desire for travel is perhaps best illustrated by the fact that more Moslems visit Europe annually now than go on pilgrimage to Mecca !

Nor did the desire to travel end simply in a journey. The better class Moslems sent their sons to Europe for education, and the universities of Germany, France, and Great Britain received many students from Moslem lands. Students one has met have given the impression of men who hated and feared the Western Powers, and despised their civilization. They studied in Europe, not because they loved or admired Western people, but because they wanted an education they could not get in their own lands. In 1919, when rebellion broke out in Egypt, an attack was made by an armed mob on a train in Upper Egypt, and eight British soldiers and others were murdered. One of the men who headed the attack and took an active part in the murder of our fellow-countrymen was a student who had spent five years in England, and had only returned to Egypt a fortnight before the tragedy occurred.

This incident throws a strange and lurid light upon our influence over young Eastern students while they are our guests in England. As we ponder over this, and the startling problem it presents, let us remember that there are thousands more students from the East in Europe to-day than there were before the War, and that our Christianity is being judged largely by the impressions these young men carry back with them to their homes and their country. A Moslem's impression of London is often that of a great pagan city, with little evidence of the presence of Christianity in our midst except on Sundays.

Nationalism and Communism

When the Armistice was signed, President Wilson propounded his theory of self-determination. The phrase was eagerly taken up by countries like Egypt, Palestine, Syria, Arabia, Mesopotamia, etc., and these countries claimed the right to lead their own lives and determine for themselves their own types of government. " Self-determination " rapidly became the watchword throughout the Moslem world from India to North Africa. To express Wilson's idea there had to be some semblance of national unity in a country, and the old religious differences of India as well as the Near East were a serious obstacle. A Moslem-Hindu alliance was formed for India, and the East began to speak of nationality as something which should be put even before religion. Indian Moslems declared that the brotherhood of Islam was more inclusive than simply " the believers," and they agreed to a union of all religions in one nation.

In Egypt the movement took on a different aspect. Here people were divided into Moslems and Copts (members of the old Christian Church of St Mark). They joined forces in a National Union to demand complete independence. A Union flag was brought forward, a red flag with a Cross and a Crescent on it in white.[1] This was surely the first time in history that the Cross and the Crescent had been seen on the same flag. It was carried in all demonstrations.

[1] See illustration facing p. 32.

Mosques and churches alike were used for political speeches, and Moslem Nationalists declared that " the Koran and the Bible are one, Jesus and Mohammed are one. The Cross and the Crescent on the one flag is proof of our national unity."

In Palestine there was a Moslem-Christian council set up to fight for liberty and the overthrow of the Balfour declaration, which made Palestine " a national home for the Jews." Feeling all through Moslem lands ran high, new thoughts were bursting their way to the surface to find expression in crude politics and impossible schemes, leading in many cases to grave disorders and riots.

Into this seething, troubled world, where races and people were groping their way towards a new day, came a strange and novel force. From the Russian Revolution there spread mysteriously through Asia such words as Bolshevism, Soviets, Communism. They were a revolutionary addition to the medley of thought and life in the East. They did not fit in with any scheme of Pan-Islamism. The atheism of Russia shocked the religious leaders of Islam, who pronounced against the Soviet idea. Nor did Communism mix with the strong Nationalism that was moving forward like a rising tide, but nevertheless Russia used all her resources to capture an unsettled East for her Soviet programme.

The heads of the Russian Government did not hesitate to use the most up-to-date methods in their propaganda work. Their aim was to stir up unrest in Asia and Africa, and messengers from Moscow flew in powerful aeroplanes, laden with propagandist pamphlets, to the most remote parts of Asia. They made use of wireless stations, aeroplanes, motors, railways, and camels in their efforts to spread their views of a world revolution. In India coloured posters appeared, and literature was distributed. Afghanistan felt the shock, and serious troubles have followed. In Palestine, on 1st May 1921, a procession was formed of Bolshevistic Jews, who circulated leaflets denouncing British capitalism and demanding a Soviet for the country. Riots followed, and many lives were lost. The Arabs took note of this strange scheme for a new world, and their leaders denounced it as anti-religious. In Egypt strikes followed in rapid succession, and Bolshevism has come to be a common word in the Arabic language.

Out of this chaos of thought there emerged two clearly defined ideas : national independence as the great aim of those who were freeing themselves from the trammels of the past ; and Islam, the old watchword of those who, in the new direction of events, feared for the Faith. The young educated Eastern mind saw in Nationalism the only hope for the future, and the religious leaders of Islam sought to graft the old Islamic branch on to the new tree of liberty. How far nationality as a basis of unity can hold together conflicting religious elements must be a study in a later chapter. How far the post-war turmoil has affected Islam as a religion only time will show, but one thing is already evident. A greater toleration is shown to-day towards Western ideas, and in particular towards Christianity. There is a willingness, and in some cases a keen desire, to study things non-Moslem, and new openings are afforded for the messengers of the Gospel.

In this chapter we have tried to show the clash between the old ways and the new. It remains to be shown how these new ideas are penetrating into the strongholds of the most conservative and old-world types of Islam. The students of the Azhar University in Cairo, described in this chapter, have petitioned the Egyptian Government asking for an improvement in their general condition, and that they should be given a better chance of taking government service. These men, whose outlook is that of the seventh century rather than the twentieth, and whose education is principally the study of Arabic and the Koran, recently went on strike. They sent a deputation to the Ministry of the Interior, and not being satisfied with the reply they received, they organized a monster demonstration and paraded the streets, shouting for their rights. Here were men, despised as "reactionaries" by Moslems of Western education, adopting modern methods of demonstration and demanding reforms! Every branch of Moslem thought and life is becoming saturated with ideas of life, liberty, progress, and rights. What will the outcome be? Will the modernism of the educated win the day, or will the masses ultimately rise to defend the old Faith and overthrow the non-Islamic influence? Will Christianity, with its living message, triumph and draw both sections together into the unity of the Kingdom of God?

CHAPTER III

FERMENT IN THE MOSLEM WORLD

In March of 1924 Hussein, then King of the Hejaz, paid a visit to his son, the Emir Abdullah, ruler of Transjordania. I had work in Amman (the capital) while the King was there, and was privileged to have a long interview with His Majesty. He was living in a large house opposite a famous old Roman forum and amphitheatre. On arrival I was passed from one official to another and introduced in turn to the King's sons, some of his generals, and an ex-minister of the late Turkish Government who had fled to Arabia for safety during the revolution under Mustapha Kemal. After waiting some time, the diplomatic secretary, a Moslem in flowing robes, who spoke very good English, announced that His Majesty would receive me. The stairs were lined with black soldiers, slaves from Africa, armed with long swords, the scabbards and hilts of which were inlaid with silver and gold. As I stepped into the presence of the King, I saw that he was an old man with a white beard and a kind and generous face. He was dressed in a most beautiful Arab costume, and his smile of welcome was typical of that rare gift of courtesy so markedly a feature of the Arab character. He took me by the hand and led me to a chair beside his own.

We talked in Arabic, and after a few minutes the question of the caliphate was raised. The King patted me on the knee and in a confidential tone said: "I will explain to you the caliphate. After Mohammed died there were four caliphs—Abu Bakr, Omar, Othman, and Ali. Since then there has not been a true caliph in the world, until I took the title. The old succession of true caliphs has been restored in my person, for a caliph must be an Arab of the Koreish tribe, a true descendant of the Prophet and the guardian of the holy place."

The Caliphate

The word caliphate has become a newspaper term since the Angora Government of Turkey drove the caliph out of Constantinople, but to understand what it means, and to see why King Hussein declared himself caliph, it is necessary for us to retrace our steps and to give a brief summary of what the caliphate stood for in Islam.

The word caliph is the English form of the Arabic word *khalifa*, which means a successor or vicegerent. It is used in the Koran for Adam, who is styled the vicegerent of the Almighty on earth (Sura 2, 28), and Sura 38, 25, says, "O David, verily we have made thee a khalifa: judge then between men with truth."

After the death of Mohammed the name caliph was used for the successors in office of Mohammed, and the caliph was vested with absolute civil and religious authority. The conditions for a true caliph laid down by the Sunni (orthodox) Moslems were that he must be a free, just, and learned man, a powerful ruler, a member of the Koreish (Mohammed's own tribe), and that he must rule in accordance with the laws of the Koran and the Traditions. The first four caliphs were by far the greatest and the most famous in the long line of successors to the Prophet. In the seventh century the capital of the caliphs was transferred from Medina to Damascus, and in the eighth century, owing to tribal wars, it was again moved to Baghdad. Then for a short time Cairo was the seat of authority.

When the Turkish Sultan, Selim I, in A.D. 1512, conquered Egypt, he sought to strengthen his power by assuming the title of caliph. He fulfilled few, if any, of the conditions laid down by the Moslem law for the caliphate : he was not elected, but usurped the office. So that from the sixteenth century the caliphate has continued as a religious power without being in any way connected with the Arab race, who claimed and still claim that in Arabia alone can a true caliph be found. This explains King Hussein's action in declaring himself caliph, for he fulfilled more of the conditions of the office than any living man. The remarkable thing is that the action of King Hussein was not endorsed by the rest of the Moslem world, and he has since been compelled to abdicate from the throne, and his son, Ali, on becoming king, renounced all claim to the caliphate. The truth is that the Sultans of Turkey from the sixteenth century had stood so strongly for the defence of orthodox Islam that they succeeded in persuading a large majority of Moslems in the world to accept them as caliphs.

The newspapers were giving last year (1924) long accounts of the war between King Hussein and the Wahabi tribe in Arabia. This little war is typical of the state of Arabia for centuries. Under Mohammed's strong personality and leadership the tribes united, but almost from the hour of his death they split up again and the old tribal feuds and wars have gone on ever since. A country divided up in this way could not give a lead to the rest of the Moslem world, whereas Turkey, united under a Sultan, and the strongest independent Moslem power, came to be looked upon increasingly by Mohammedans in other countries as the rock and strength of their Faith, and in course of time the position usurped by Selim I was conceded by other Moslem lands. By the nineteenth century, when Moslems were seeking to reform and revive Islam because of the growing influence of the West, they naturally turned to Turkey, not to Arabia, for leadership. Countries under British control were the most active in promoting what was called the Caliphate Movement, and its strongest supporters were found, not in Turkey, but in India, where the Moslems looked upon the Sultan of Turkey as their pope, the head of their Faith, and the centre of Moslem unity throughout the world.

Islam in the Turkish Republic

In the previous chapter we have seen how Mustapha Kemal, after his victory over the Greeks, was looked upon by the whole Moslem world as the saviour of Islam, the hope of the Faith. When Turkey dethroned the Sultan in 1922 and set up a republic, Moslem leaders agreed with her action, as the Sultan, by signing the Treaty of Sèvres, had forfeited his right to be head of the first Moslem power. But the establishing of a republic involved many changes. The capitulations [1] had been abolished, and a new civil code was badly needed. Mustapha was placed on the horns of a dilemma. If he retained the old Moslem law, there would still need to be a caliph, who would be a relative of the deposed Sultan, and therefore a grave danger to the new republic and its president. On the other hand, he could modernize Turkey, do away with the office of caliph, and make the Angora Assembly the centre of authority in the State.

The young educated Turks from the days of the revolution in 1908, when Abdul Hamid was dethroned, had shown little regard for Islam. They had tolerated the old Faith and used it to further their political ambitions, but they were mostly agnostic or infidel in their attitude to religion. The object of the Angora Government was to lift Turkish culture to the level of the West, whether at the cost of Islam or no. The republic had sprung out of a new national movement that was purely Turkish. The old Pan-Islamic scheme did not enter into its calculations, and the new government represented a lay movement in which the religious leaders played little or no part. The " republicans " thought of themselves as Turks first and Moslems afterwards.

[1] Grants made by successive Sultans to Christian nations, conferring rights and privileges in favour of their subjects resident or trading in Ottoman dominions.

People who had not followed the trend of events in Turkey were amazed to learn that in the new republic the Mohammedan religion was no longer to be the official State religion in the old sense of the word, when political power and religious authority were centred in one man, the Sultan. This did not mean, of course, that the Moslem faith was under a ban, but that religion in Turkey had ceased to be the chief factor in the politics of the country. Religion henceforth was no longer to be a phase of national life, supported by the State, guiding and dominating it as in pre-war days. It was to be purely the concern of the individual. To make this crystal clear the following motions were brought forward in the Turkish parliament and carried :

(a) The absolute abolition of the caliphate.
(b) The abolition of the Ministry of Wakfs or religious endowments.
(c) The abolition of all governmental religious foundations.
(d) The deportation within ten days of all members of the caliph's family and the withdrawal from them of Turkish citizenship.

This could only mean one thing—the Turkish Republic had of its own free will given up the position of influence which it had held in Islam for five hundred years, the position of " Defender of the Faith of Islam." It sacrificed the enormous prestige which the Sultans as heads of the Faith had always held in the Mohammedan world. The Turkish Sultan as Caliph had been the Commander of the Faithful,

Chief of all Believers, Pope of Islam and Bearer of the Mantle of the Prophet himself. Yet so completely had opinion changed that the caliph, when he left Constantinople, was the butt of scorn and ridicule in the comic picture papers of Turkey !

However much Moslems may say that this is purely a political move which does not affect Islam as a religion, certain outstanding facts go to prove that Turkey's attitude towards the caliph has dealt a severe blow at Islam as a whole. It is merely an indication of the attitude of many Turks towards a Faith which they appear no longer to hold. It marks a definite cleavage between Church and State. One Turk put it this way : " This is the best thing Turkey ever did. We are becoming modern and we are cutting loose from religion." There seems to be no doubt that a large section of the people have lost their reverence for the Koran and the caliph, and the Koran has been spoken of in the newspapers as out-of-date. One Turkish editor, more outspoken perhaps than others, referring to the protests from different parts of the Moslem world against Turkish action, said : " No thinking Turk can be a Moslem to-day."

It is clear that this action on the part of Turkey is not a personal attack upon the caliph as an individual ; it is a blow to all that the caliphate stood for. The expulsion of the caliph meant also the overthrow of Islamic religious courts of law and religious schools. It was in fact a revolt against Mohammedan law, as something out of date.

In order to understand to some extent what a revolution is represented in Turkey's present attitude to the caliphate, let us remember what was the position up to 1914. Then, for a Turk to give up the Moslem faith, was an offence punishable by death : Turkey stood before the world as the champion of Islam, and the religious leaders of the country largely dominated all her policy : the Mohammedan law of the land was based on the Koran, a book Moslems claim to be heaven-sent, verbally inspired, the absolute word of God and the final revelation of God to man.

Turkish students of history would appear to doubt whether Turkey gained anything by becoming Moslem. Some are inclined to think that she would have been a stronger nation to-day if she had adhered to her old pagan faith and never embraced Islam at all. There is certain evidence for this opinion in the prayers used by Turkish soldiers during the War. Mr C. F. Riggs, on the authority of *The Near East*, contributed the following to *The Moslem World* in January 1919 :

A little over two years ago a prayer specially drawn up by Enver Pasha, the Turkish Minister of War, was ordered to be recited every night by each soldier in the Turkish army. This remarkable document contained no reference whatever to Islam and is a deliberate attempt to turn back the hands of the clock to pre-Moslem times. The translation follows— " Almighty God, grant the Turks health and unite all the Brethren in the benevolence of the Sultan. That Thy power may be glorified grant us the favour of the White Wolf. Thou, Young Turan, thou beloved Fatherland, we beseech Thee to show us thy path. Our great ancestor Abhouz calls us ! "

D

In pre-war days prayers were offered for the Sultan, as caliph, in mosques throughout the Turkish Empire and in countries beyond. When the caliph left Constantinople a Turkish official was asked, " In whose name will the prayers be now offered, as there is no caliph ? " and he replied, " In the name of the Turkish republican government."

Another fact is clear—that as far as Turkey is concerned the Pan-Islamic ideal is dead. It has been killed by the intense individualistic type of nationalism adopted by Turkey. The theory of Móhammedanism does involve a type of government with the head of the State also the head of the Faith and God's representative on earth. In orthodox Islam it seems impossible to conceive of a State separated from religion. Of course this theory had never worked in lands where non-Moslem powers ruled, but in countries under purely Moslem government, such as Turkey, Church and State were one. It can therefore be claimed that this new Turkish Republic signifies the overthrow of the very principles for which Mohammed stood and a negation of the idealism of Abu Bakr when he first set out to conquer the world. The Caliphate question therefore is likely to split Islam in twain.

When the news of Turkish action was cabled through the world in 1922 Islam was staggered. Mustapha Kemal, their hope and saviour, had betrayed them and thrown over the Faith. One Moslem writer spoke of it as " one of the gravest moments in the world's history " and said that it had " thrown Islam into a ferment."

Many Moslems attributed Turkey's action to Bolshevist influence. To prove this they pointed to the way Mustapha Kemal had disendowed religion. Disendowment, they angrily declared, was but another word for confiscation of religious funds. The fact that the jewels of the princes and princesses were stolen from them before they were banished made feeling more bitter. And when it was known that the chairman of the committee which drafted the Bill deposing the Sultan, abolishing the caliphate, and confiscating the belongings of the innocent members of the caliph's family, was none other than the pro-Bolshevik extremist, Youni Hadi, people declared that Turkey was under the thumb of Russia.

There is probably some truth in this point of view, and one must take account of Moscow influence at Angora, but so far Turkey seems to have been saved from Bolshevism in its Russian form by its new and intense patriotism, by a fear of possible Russian aggression, and by the fact that the great mass of people in Turkey, especially of the peasant class, are still strong Moslems, and therefore opposed to anything that would set up a Soviet on atheistic lines.

The Caliphate Movement in India

Moslem India was probably more hardly hit by Turkey's treatment of the caliph than most countries because she had so persistently fought for the caliphate. In 1912 an Indian delegation came to England to protest to Sir Edward Grey against the abandonment of Turkey by England. When Mohammed Ali met on that visit a certain number of Press representatives and members of the House of Commons at the Hotel Cecil, he proclaimed the unity of Indian Moslems with Turkey. Felix Valyi in *The Islamic Review* says : " For years the Moslem leaders of India reproached the British rulers with undermining the position of the Sultan-Caliph, with making common cause with the Sultan's enemies ; and after all the Turks themselves got rid of an institution which has existed for six centuries, and which was for so long the rallying point of Orthodox Islam."

Attitude of Moslems to Turkey

Moslem opinion here divides into two. The liberal type of Islam represented by the Mohammedan college at Aligarh in India, disturbed as it is, sees the possibilities of a reformation of Islam through Turkish policy, but perhaps takes too little notice of the fact that Turkey has dealt a serious blow at Islam by placing her national interests above those of her Faith. *The Islamic Review* for April 1924 contains the following remarkable utterance :

The Holy Prophet never considered himself infallible ; he admitted his own errors. Why should a true Moslem accept some theologian of the past centuries as a supreme and infallible authority ? Why refuse to the greatest living man in the Moslem world, to Mustapha Kemal Pasha, the right to give a new interpretation of the science of controversy ?

Few, if any, of the religious leaders of the Azhar University in Cairo would agree with this liberal interpretation of the problem. They stand for the old conservative and orthodox Islam, and they were among the first to issue a manifesto " denouncing the invalid action of Angora." A Moslem writer in Cairo says :

There is no other path to reassure the Moslem world concerning the future of Islam (and especially since the Turkish republic has abandoned the task of caring for the general Moslem welfare), except the execution of this idea, namely, that of calling a Pan-Islamic Council to deliberate on all matters affecting the caliphate, which is the sole prop of Islam.

We have seen Moslems of Turkey shaking themselves free from what they look upon as hindrances to progress, the shock of the Moslem world on learning the news, the pathetic appeals of the old-time religious leaders for a council to find a new caliph—but who should it be ? King Hussein, who was proclaimed caliph by a section of Arabia, has, as we have seen, already been deposed. In Egypt some advocate that King Fouad should be made caliph, while in India some aspire to seeing Aman-ullah Khan, Amir of Afghanistan, the Defender of the Faithful. One thing is clear. No one man will command the allegiance of the Moslem world as a whole. The Arabs will never yield their claim to the Amir of Afghanistan, and the tribes of North Africa would scorn the idea of accepting King Fouad of Egypt as caliph. The semblance of unity that once existed is gone. Turkey's action has let loose new thoughts, and already in Cairo at least one Moslem daily paper argues in favour of the Kemalist policy and declares that religion ought to have nothing to do with the State.

Christianity in the Turkish Republic

Turkey under a republic has a far better scheme of education than ever before. A new liberty has been granted to the Press. Women are taking their place in national affairs and are even demanding votes. Religious fanaticism has disappeared to a large extent, but at present it is being replaced by a national bigotry which causes everything foreign to be unpopular. By Turkish law, for instance, merchants must appoint Turks in their offices.

The trend of recent events points to a wider liberty than before in many directions, but so far this has not touched Christian institutions. No boy is allowed to attend any religious exercise in a school unless he is a member of the denomination of the institution. There seems no doubt that the Turks view Christianity as a foreign body, and the Great War embittered them not only against the Greek Church but against Christianity as a whole. They fear a strong Christian force in their midst for two reasons : they think Eastern Churches will become again the tools of Western Powers and will be used for political ends to curtail Turkish liberty, and they fear missions lest large numbers of Moslems should go over to the Christian Faith. It may have been some such reason as this last that led the Turks to wipe out all the American Congregational churches in Anatolia. Before the War there were sixty-five churches with growing congregations and pastors, and in the most cold-blooded manner the people were massacred, pastors slain, and churches demolished. Change of religion in Turkey in pre-war days was made impossible by law. The penalty for anyone leaving Islam to become Christian was death, and so far this law appears to be still operative. If Turkey is true to the principles on which she has founded the republic she must make religion not only a matter for the individual but also a question of conscience, and leave men and women free to choose their faith for themselves. The new liberty that Turkey claims for herself nationally she cannot ultimately deny to the individual members of the nation.

Turkey is pulling down her own house to build another. She is touchy about any foreign interference, and suspicious of Christian missions. The educated men of Turkey to-day owe an immense debt to the missionary educational work of the past. Sooner or later things must become stable again, and in the wider vision of freedom, the increase of education, and the desire for progress, the present hindrances to Christian missions will disappear, and a new day dawn for a land that has for centuries stood for the persecution of the Christian Faith and the massacre of its followers.

In the meantime— what ? There is to-day a growing band of secret disciples, men who have found a new hope in life through Jesus Christ. Here is the testimony of one missionary who met many such :

Many of these secret believers are from the higher walks of life. When making a round of calls I met two brothers, one a Pasha and member of the old Ottoman parliament, the other the Governor of an important province. The Pasha, being the elder, took the lead in the conversation and suddenly began to speak on religious subjects. There were not less than twenty other Moslem men present, and the Pasha was speaking with such earnestness and conviction. I said, " You appear to know our book ? " " I know it very well," he said. " You never found anything bad in it, did you ? " I enquired. " On the contrary I found but one theme like a scarlet thread running through the entire book—' This is life eternal that they might know Thee the only true God and Jesus Christ whom Thou hast sent.' That is what the Bible teaches, and to have eternal life is to know our Lord and Saviour Jesus Christ." " Are there many like you ? " I queried incredulous. " Many," was the reply. " And where ? " I asked. " Everywhere," was the answer. Within a few days a group of Moslem women called, and soon the topic of conversation was the knowledge the Pasha had of the Christians' Book, for the men present that day had evidently discussed it at home. But a surprise came to me when every woman present asserted she possessed a Bible and read it also.

Bolshevism may seek to undermine religion, the law of apostasy be applied to Islamic lands, converts punished and Christians massacred, but the leaven of the Gospel wins its way into the hearts and lives of those who in sincerity are seekers after the Truth.

Three forces are contending for Turkey to-day. Moscow is undoubtedly trying to gain an open door into Eastern Europe through Constantinople, and Bolshevists keep up a strong pressure upon the leaders of Turkish life and thought. Mustapha Kemal and his colleagues, with patriotic and national ideals, are seeking to build up a free, strong, and educated Turkey on modern lines. The old conservative party is by no means dead ; they dare not denounce the present government, because it would mean death to anyone who did so, but they wait and silently watch for an opportunity of overthrowing the Angora Government and introducing again a Sultan-Caliph who would reside at Constantinople.

The republic is too young for one to offer any prophecy as to the future of Turkey, but whatever happens the education which these last few years have meant cannot be lost, and the people must move forward to a larger liberty which will bring with it the right of Turkish subjects to choose religion for themselves, the right to become Christian if they wish. The open door of the Gospel, such a feature of Islam to-day, is strangely closed in the most progressive country in the Moslem world.

CHAPTER IV

ISLAM IN INDIA

THE mysterious Nile in its annual rise and fall was worshipped by the Egyptians. Floodtide and harvest were the work of the river-god, and great care was taken to propitiate this deity. If he were angry the blessing of the flood was turned into a curse and disaster followed. One year the flood rose higher and higher; the average rise of the water, about thirty feet, was reached and passed and still the torrents poured down over the cataracts. The banks burst in places, crops were ruined, houses destroyed, and many lives lost. The water came tearing, raging down carrying destruction in all directions. The people believed their god was angry and they bowed to the inevitable storm and prayed for it to pass. Many years later British engineers harnessed those floods and brought the surplus water on to dry and uncultivated land, thus turning what might have meant ruin into prosperity.

The rise of Islam in the world is one of the Church's lost opportunities. The Christian forces of Arabia [1] might have harnessed all the virile character and zeal

[1] There is evidence of Christianity in Arabia at quite an early date. Five Arabian bishops are said to have attended the Council of Nicæa in A.D. 325.

of the Arab on to the great work of winning the world for Christ, but when the flood of religious fervour came the Church failed utterly to cope with the situation, and a great torrent that carried with it untold sufferings for millions of people was poured out on to the world.

In A.D. 1001 the storm broke over India. Through the Khyber Pass there swarmed from Afghanistan a Moslem army which met and defeated the King of Lahore near Peshawar. The Moslem war-cry was "For the Faith, kill, kill," and the age-long pride of India was humbled in a series of crushing defeats. One beaten king proclaimed himself unworthy to reign, and amid the grief of a stricken people mounted the funeral pyre and burned himself to death in the sight of his followers. Time after time came the Mohammedans, and in each invasion they devastated some new district and spread red ruin through the land. The wealth and culture of centuries disappeared under the flood of an invading foe, and India sank into despair. Unable to stem the tide the people bowed to the inevitable and prayed to all the gods for mercy.

The sixteenth century has well been described as one of the turning-points in history. While Selim I was annexing Egypt and usurping the title of Caliph, Luther was propounding his theses at Wittenberg. While German troops were pillaging Rome, a Moslem army was besieging Vienna, and Akbar the Great was ruling in Agra while Elizabeth was finally freeing England from papal domination. Akbar reigned under the title Kaisar-i-Hind, and four centuries later British sovereigns use as their Indian title this title of the great Akbar, the greatest in many ways of Moslem rulers in India. Akbar was the son of a fugitive emperor ; he was born in the desert and brought up as a nomad, yet he caught some of the inspiration of the great movements that were shaking the world. Europe was in the throes of a struggle for new liberty, freedom and civilization, and Akbar was the first Moslem ruler in India to stand for the principle of toleration for all. His empire was to be neither Moslem nor Hindu, but Indian.

Contact with the West was established, and British merchants found their way to the court of Akbar. The story of India for the next three hundred years is one of the growing influence of Europe upon Eastern life and trade, the exploitation of India's wealth to swell the dividends of foreign companies, and among Indians themselves a deepening race hatred between Hindus and Mohammedans. The establishing of British rule has in many ways meant the realization of the ideals of Akbar, though scarcely in the manner he would have wished, and the development, education and peace of a hitherto distracted land are due to the policy of freedom and " toleration for all " carried out by British administration. This policy has in turn called out new forces in Islam in India and these we must now study.

Extent of Moslem Influence

In order to understand the position of Moslems in India let us first of all look at their relative strength and location in relation to the rest of the population.

The map of India is like a triangle with its apex in the south and its base in the north. The frontier on the north-west is intersected by great passes through the mountains like the outspread fingers of a man's hand. It was, as we have seen, through these gorges that the Moslems poured in their invasion of India. The northern provinces thus were the first to suffer, and it is there to-day that we find the Moslems in strongest force. The North-West Frontier Province, bordering on Afghanistan, is mainly Mohammedan, and the population of Kashmir adjoining it is seventy-seven per cent Moslem. All along the base of the triangle through the United Provinces, Bihar, Bengal, and Assam, Islam is strongly represented. As one travels south the number of Moslems decreases, and the Hindus predominate.

Moslem invasions, terrible though they were, never succeeded in the conversion of India as a whole to Islam, and the followers of the Prophet are to-day a minority of the population—seventy millions out of India's three hundred and nineteen millions. It will perhaps help us, however, to appreciate their numbers to remember that there are more Moslems in India than in any other country in the world. Bengal, for example, on the north-east, has a larger Moslem population than Arabia, Egypt and Persia put together, and in no less than ten provinces of India the Moslem population numbers over a million in each.

It should not be taken from what has been said that this enormous Moslem community in India is due simply to military campaigns and forced conversions. The sword alone is no adequate explanation of the presence of so large a Moslem element. We ask, then, what was it that appealed to non-Moslem Indians? It is true that for eight centuries all the power of a Moslem government was used without restraint to bring India under the yoke of Islam. In some areas it signally failed and in others it succeeded. The fact is that Islam was never able to break through the Hindu caste system,[1] but where Moslems met outcastes there is another story to tell. The outcaste had little, if anything, to gain by warring against Moslems. On the contrary, Moslems came proclaiming a common brotherhood within the House of Islam, deliverance from Hindu tyranny and caste contempt, and the outcastes were offered social recognition and land rights where they had been but serfs under Hindu rule. So far so good, and the reader at this stage may imagine that at last these people were on the road to progress and freedom, but the first half of the nineteenth century reveals what has so frequently happened in Moslem history. The high-sounding words of brotherhood and equality seem to lose their force under a stagnant system of religion, and we see Islam in India declining in power and decaying in vitality.

Reform Movements in the House of Islam

The great turning-point in Moslem life in India in modern times dates from the Mutiny of 1857.

[1] Hindu society is divided into about 2500 classes or castes. Rigid rules separate one caste from another, so that there is no inter-marriage and no sharing of a common meal. The outcastes, who number about fifty-two millions in India to-day, are below all the castes. They are often called "the untouchables," and are despised and shunned by all caste people.

For centuries the Moslems of North India have known very little of the world outside. The mullahs (religious leaders) have provided all the religious teaching required, and have gained a complete control over the minds of the less educated people. When missionaries opened schools they found their chief opponents were the mullahs, who everywhere discouraged the people from sending their children to mission schools. Even when the Government established secular schools the Moslems were slow to make use of them; thus it came about that schools were for the most part patronized by the Hindu and Christian population rather than by the Moslems. Thus Government posts were filled mainly by Hindus and Christians, who generally took the lead. The Moslems awoke with alarm. The Indian Mutiny had opened their eyes to see the perilous position in which they were placed, in a minority and surrounded by people of other religions. They also realized for the first time the value of Western education and the need of reform.

Syed Ahmad Khan, who came of an ancient and noble family, headed a new movement for reformation within the House of Islam. He studied Western literature and developed a rationalistic form of thought which he tried to graft on to the Islamic stock. He used often to say, " All the religious learning in Mohammedan libraries is of no avail," and he founded a society for the study of Western science. He was slandered and persecuted, but he held firmly to his principles. By establishing English schools he sought to introduce into Islam the culture of the

West. The climax to his educational efforts came when he opened the Mohammedan College at Aligarh in 1875. He sought to do for the Moslem youth of India what Oxford and Cambridge had done for Englishmen. From this college there grew up a new Islam in India, the influence of which has been felt in every Moslem country in the world. "Aligarh" has now become a name that denotes something more than a college. It stands for a movement on progressive and modern lines. Thus from the Indian Mutiny there dates a new revival of Moslem learning and influence in India. As the influence of Aligarh spread, Educational Conferences for the Moslems of India were held annually in different parts of the country, and in recent years a conference of Moslem women has met alongside the men's conference to study education for women and girls.

This movement, which began with strong rational-istic tendencies, has in some respects modified its programme although it has stuck loyally to its first ideals of enlightenment and progress. Rationalism has been dropped. In fact Syed Ahmad Khan never succeeded in persuading his co-religionists to follow him in this, and the religious teaching now given in the College is of a more orthodox type.

Reactionary movements in opposition to Aligarh are a factor to be reckoned with, and even to-day many of the mullahs are anxious to keep the people as long as possible under their sway and oppose all education and any sort of reform. Even infant welfare and inoculation, one missionary writes, are

A FAMOUS MOSQUE IN NORTH INDIA

Akbar's Mosque at Fatehpur Sikri near Agra, whose size and architectural splendour make it one of the most impressive mosques in the world, was built to celebrate the victories of Akbar the Great (see p. 60).

resisted by the mullahs, who still adopt the old cry that they are opposed to " Holy Islam."

But in spite of such reactionary influences the Moslem community as a whole in North India is making progress in material and social life ; while in religious life many are prepared to study the claims of Christianity, and some have openly identified themselves with the Christian Church.

The Aligarh Movement has found expression in a remarkable way in literature. Idiomatic translations of the Koran are being used. The use of fiction to advocate religious and social ideas is rapidly extending. Liberal views are promoted through the periodical magazine or the newspaper. "Modern Moslem literature is in India a political force to be reckoned with—a self-conscious and organized force. For the last ten years a distinct type of political literature has been flooding the country. Politics are given to the public in the form of poetry, drama and fiction, and always the politics of Islam. Political and religious antagonism merge, as throughout the story of Islam they have ever merged." [1]

We have seen Islam on its modernist side represented by Aligarh. Let us now look at another great movement, the Ahmadiya Movement. Mysticism long ago found a home among Moslems, and in 1879 Mirza Ghulam Ahmad, of the village of Qadian in the Punjab, began to propound to his Moslem brethren his new teaching, in which there was a good deal of mysticism. His teaching was chiefly based upon his personal claims. He declared himself to be

[1] *Christian Literature in Moslem Lands*, pp. 26–27.

the Christian Messiah, the Mohammedan Mahdi, and the final incarnation expected by the Hindus.   His claim at once brought him into conflict with orthodox Islam.   The Mahdi (the final successor of the Prophet) was to be a man of blood ; how then could Mirza Ghulam Ahmad combine in his own person the character of Jesus, a man of peace, with that of the Mahdi ?   He got over this by declaring that the traditions about the Mahdi were forgeries, and he was to be a man of peace, not war.   The Ahmadiya Movement is remarkable for the way it turned the attention of Mohammedans to the study of Jesus Christ.   It came at a time when Syed Ahmad Khan was developing Western education at Aligarh, and this new and self-styled Messiah sought to find a middle way between the irresistible onrush of the Western rationalism of Syed Ahmad Khan, and the impossible orthodoxy of the old conservative religious leaders.

It is clear, therefore, that no one movement is typical of all Moslem India.   Each leader impresses a larger or smaller group of people, and the ideas put forward have an undoubted influence upon the life of the whole community.   Thus we see different and contending lines of thought all exercising an influence and leading the Moslem population toward an unknown goal.   Western thought widens the outlook of people generally and makes for greater toleration ; the mysticism of the Ahmadiyas turns people's attention to the spiritual side of religion ; and the old orthodox teachers, who denounce both ideas as subversive of Islam, seek to keep Moslems true to the primitive type

of religion as seen in Arabia in the early days of
their faith.

Movements among Women

Perhaps the most hopeful aspect of Indian life
to-day is the awakening of her womanhood. Irresistible forces are breaking down the barriers of seclusion
behind which the Moslem women of India live. Increasingly women are beginning to be swept into
the current of modern life. Most striking of all
is the widespread and vehement demand for the
education of girls. Educated Moslems are seeking
to reform the customs, such as polygamy and harem
life, which have so vitally affected the moral life
of Moslems in India in times past. The leaders
of thought admit that these things stand in the
way of racial, material, social and religious development. Some leading Mohammedans have put
their modern ideas into practice and have broken
the Islamic ordinance of the veil, and appear in
public with their wives and daughters in European
dress.

These movements are in no sense the outcome
of orthodox Islam. They are due partly to the
liberalizing tendencies of the Aligarh Movement and
partly to the impact of Western Christianity through
missionary enterprise. With an increasing body of
educated women in India this demand for women's
rights is becoming a national problem. In August
1924 a large and representative gathering of Indian
ladies was held at Simla, when the following resolution was passed :—

This meeting of Indian women, belonging to different parts of India, records its very strong opinion that the disability of women to stand as candidates for the Legislatures be removed forthwith, and that the rules, under the Government of India Act, be amended accordingly.

In several provinces in recent years women have been given the municipal franchise, and as members of local bodies they have been doing very useful work.

It must not, however, be thought that all Moslem women are becoming modern. In the Punjab, for example, only a few outstanding Moslem women take part in national movements. These strive to keep informed about Indian matters and hold meetings to represent women's views on social and national affairs. They seek to help their less educated sisters, the great bulk of whom are as yet untouched in this way. It is probably true to say that women are the most conservative class in the community. On the whole they adhere strictly to the rules of their Faith and cling tenaciously to the old customs and superstitions. The encouraging sign, however, is the growing body of educated women who are seeking to emancipate the womanhood of their land.

Moslems and Non-Moslems

It was evident from the first that education, a new outlook on the world, and a more liberal attitude to non-Moslems in India must eventually lead to a new attitude to politics. Moslems were, by the forces let loose through these new movements, beginning to think in terms not only of their own co-religionists, but of India as a whole. With this attitude came not only a new race consciousness, but also a new national consciousness. The ideal of the leaders was the unity of India, and their greatest difficulty was the heritage of past wars, the clash between Hindu and Moslem. A Hindu-Moslem Alliance was formed to try to bridge the gulf. How difficult it has been is seen from the continual strife between Hindus and Moslems, but whether it is sincere and permanent or not, the fact that such an alliance is at all possible must have a profound significance for religion throughout India.

"The All-India Congress, made up of Hindus and Mohammedans alike, was united in making Mr Gandhi director of the Nationalist Movement. It would be interesting to hear Mohammed express his mind on the acceptance of a Hindu as the absolute politica leader of seventy million Mohammedans in India!

"The resolutions of the Congress set forth as one of its goals the 'consolidation of unity among all races and communities of India, whether Hindu, Moslem, Sikh, Parsi, Christian or Jew.'" [1] Many who know India well affirm that this alliance is only superficial and unreal. But what has the leadership of Mr Gandhi meant for Islam? It is admitted that "from the first Mr Gandhi's teaching has consciously been influenced by that of Christ, for whom his admiration has long been the almost dominating feature of his spiritual life, and probably the external character of his daily activity has been modelled also upon Him." [2]

[1] R. E. Speer's *Report on India and Persia*, p. 168.
[2] *Ibid.*, p. 120.

Robert E. Speer, in his *Report* already quoted, gives a striking example of the fusion that is coming about among all classes. " One day," he says, " on a dining-car on the Great Indian Peninsular Railway we counted at the tables two Mohammedan men, two Sikhs, several high caste Hindu women with the religious mark on their foreheads, several Parsis, four or five Eurasians, Hindu men of various castes, some British officers and Tommies, and two English women. We watched the Mohammedan and the high caste Hindu men and women and saw them refuse none of the food. The Mohammedans even took the bacon which was served with the omelette. A few years ago a dozen cleavages, now wholly ignored, would have cut this company into fragments. The British would have had one or two dining-cars of their own, and the Indians would have separated into half a dozen groups." [1] This fusion is breaking down barriers and giving to India a wide vision of the future. It is a fusion of social, political and religious thought, and when one remembers how largely its success has depended on one man, and that that man has taken Christ as his pattern and ideal, we shall understand what the Rev. W. E. S. Holland meant when he said, " India has made Christ Lord of thought, but she has not yet made Him Lord of life." The missionary task is certainly great—to turn this new mentality of India into a living and heart service for our Lord.

The tendencies of educated Moslems in India have been in recent years mainly rationalistic, but a new

[1] *Ibid.*, pp. 142-3.

spiritual note has been introduced into national life
and thought that has made India, and Moslem India
too, study the Man Christ Jesus. The sharp edges of
religious fanaticism get rubbed off through contact
with other faiths, and missionaries report that there
is a new willingness to listen to the Gospel, and that
even the old orthodox Moslems show less bigotry than
before and a greater readiness to discuss the Christian
message. These efforts for unity may be doomed to
failure, and in fact the reports of Hindu-Moslem riots
seem to point that way, but in this very attempt
to unite conflicting races the missionaries find one
strong reason for their work and labour. Loving
India as they do, they want to see her come to Christ,
because they are convinced that it is only through
Christ that a solid and permanent unity can ever
be achieved.

India and the Caliphate.

While this alliance with non-Moslem faiths has been
pressed for political purposes, the leaders of Islam
have not been slow to see the need of safeguarding
their own faith. An All-India Moslem League has
been formed. It takes an extremist position in
politics and it has bitterly attacked England on what
it calls the Caliphate question. Prior to the war
Indian Moslems upbraided England for taking side
with Turkey's enemies.[1] This was emphasized in
the Tripoli - Italian war. England was said to
be hostile to the Caliphate and to be seeking
the destruction of Turkey, and with it all that

[1] See p. 51.

Turkey stood for in the world of Islam. The Pan-Islamic Movement found its most ardent supporters in India.

In December 1921 the All-India Moslem Congress passed a resolution declaring its irrevocable decision not to enter into any compromise or settlement with Government about Home Rule for India without the settlement of the Caliphate question. A second resolution was carried congratulating Mustapha Kemal Pasha and the Turks on their success, and assuring the Turkish nation of India's sympathy and support. Here Indian Moslems took their stand. How far they sincerely believed in Turkey as the unifying centre of Islam it is difficult to say. The Caliphate cry was a good stick with which to beat England, and it was used with great effect. Imagine then the shock of India and the All-India Moslem League when they learned that not England but Turkey herself had driven the Caliph out of house and home, caricatured him in the comic press, and robbed him of family possessions and jewels. Moslem Indians saw their dreams of a great Islamic League, stretching from Eastern Europe to Western Asia and India, vanishing from sight like a hazy mist on a summer morning. They saw Pan-Islamism practically dead and a new nationality in Moslem lands on non-Islamic lines taking its place. India had demanded of England freedom for Turkey. Turkey had taken her own freedom and liberty, but it was national in aim, not Islamic, and it refused to recognize India's right to any say in Turkey's affairs. The Caliph, rejected by his countrymen, sought refuge in Europe, and his lack of means became a matter of serious concern to many Indian Moslems who refused to agree to Mustapha Kemal Pasha's high-handed action. The Nizam of Hyderabad came to the rescue and offered the deposed Caliph a life pension of £3600 per annum. This is the more remarkable because the Nizam strongly opposed the pro-Caliphate extremists in India, and when Turkey declared war on England in 1914, the Nizam called upon the Moslems of India to support the British Government.

Moslem India and the Gospel

Nothing is more significant in India to-day than the religious background to all the agitation and political ferment. Every movement in India has been soaked in religion, and the leaders on both the Hindu and the Mohammedan sides have given a new prominence to the teaching and character of Jesus Christ. The spiritual longings of the people are a great quest for God, and it is significant that while these new forces are shaking India, many thousands of the people are finding the goal of their spiritual aspirations in the Christian faith. Missionary work of over a hundred years has succeeded in permeating the country with the message of the Gospel.

Can the Gospel triumph in and through all this ferment? We have seen India facing Christwards, thousands of outcastes seeking baptism, the educated setting out on a great quest for something that will save and unite their land, the women becoming a national force and rising to make their unique contribution to a new India. In this day of need what have we to give them ? The missionary work of the past century has profoundly changed India's life, thought and outlook. The conversion of India is no longer the dreamy ideal of a mere enthusiast, but a practical proposition before the Christian Church.

When we speak of the Christianization of India let us not forget that *Moslem* India is in a very real sense an unoccupied field. Moslem evangelization has been looked upon as unfruitful and difficult. And yet where Christian teaching has been given there have been thrilling results. The conversions from Islam, especially in Northern India, have been continuous during all the years since the death of Henry Martyn. In the north, especially in the Punjab and the North-West Frontier Province, every congregation has a representation from Moslem ranks. Some of the churches have a majority of their membership gathered from among Moslems. In a few cases there have been movements among Moslems towards Christianity and a considerable number have come out at one time. Perhaps the most striking fact of all is this, that among the native pastors and Christian preachers and teachers in North India there are at least two hundred who were once followers of Islam. In the Punjab the converts number several thousand. The missionaries at the Bogra Conference (1924) estimated the number of baptized Moslems in Bengal at sixteen thousand. One thing is clear : there is far more liberty to preach Christ and confess Christ openly in India to-day than ever before, and missionaries are now free to carry out every method of the Church's great enterprise. The door is wide open, and what the Christian has sought in prayer for a hundred years has happened ; Moslems are not only accessible geographically or politically, but they are also mentally open to Christian influence.

We have mentioned that one of the great assets in Islam is its brotherhood. A Hindu or an outcaste coming into the House of Islam forgets all caste drawbacks, social inequalities disappear, and the convert is welcomed as a brother. The problem before us in India—one that the Indian Church alone can solve—is how to bind Hindu and Moslem together into a real unity within the Christian Church. In areas where Hinduism prevails, the Moslem convert is often looked upon with suspicion, and racial bitterness carried over into the Church is a barrier to progress in Moslem evangelization. The Church, now so strongly established in India, must become a home, a fellowship and a brotherhood for the Moslem seeker after Truth. This need is particularly urgent to-day when Moslems are becoming increasingly conscious of a deeper need than is met in their own Faith. The ethical standards of Arabia in the seventh century no longer satisfy. Voices in the press and on the platform advocate the abolition of the veil, purdah, polygamy and child marriage. The soil of their hearts has been broken up by the ploughshare of God, and the people are ready for a message that is dynamic, a Gospel that is indeed the power of God, a religion that expresses God in terms of constraining love.

Robert E. Speer writes: Many persons mistake the way in which the conversion of India will be brought about. I believe it will take place at last wholesale, just as our own ancestors were converted. The country will have Christian instruction infused into it in every way by direct missionary education, and indirectly by books of various sorts, through the public papers, through conversations with Europeans, and in all the conceivable ways in which knowledge is communicated. Then at last when society is completely saturated with Christian knowledge, and public opinion has taken a decided turn that way, they will come over by thousands.[1]

It is easy to say the Church's task is set and clear, but if all India is to be won for Christ every race and religion must be " saturated " with the Gospel, and here lies a danger and a menace. We have seen the changes, opportunities and openings among Moslems. We read of a new willingness among the most orthodox Moslems in India to listen to the Christian message. But how can they hear without a preacher? The great majority of missionaries even in areas where Moslems form a large percentage of the population have given their time and strength almost entirely to non-Moslem work, and although the great national, social and religious movements in India are reacting on Islam and making its followers daily more accessible to the Gospel, yet there are very few missionaries with either the time or the experience with which to tackle this problem. A great movement towards Christianity on the part of a large section of Indians, which leaves Islam untouched and unevangelized, is

[1] *Report on India and Persia*, p. 53.

fraught with grave danger for India's future. The task *is* set, but it involves our giving, in this day of Moslem awakening, the best we have, until the age-long feuds of races and religions find their solution in the unity of the Kingdom of God and India can say, " We are all one—in Christ Jesus."

CHAPTER V

WHAT THE MOSLEM READS

IT is related by Moslem writers that when the leader of the Arab armies conquered Persia he wrote to Omar, the Caliph, and asked him what he should do with the books which had been found in the literature of Persia, whether he should keep them or send them to Mecca. Omar replied, " Cast them into the rivers, for if in these books there is a guidance of life then we have a still better guidance in the Book of God [the Koran], and if, on the contrary, there is in them that which will lead us astray, then God protect us from them." So according to these instructions some books were cast into the river and others into the fire, and the philosophy of Persia was thus lost to the world.

This incident is typical of the spirit in which the early Moslems regarded literature in the countries they conquered.

After the death of Mohammed, the Koran was given to the world as the Uncreated and Eternal Word and as a standing miracle, not only of sound doctrine, but of literary style and language. With one book dominating the life and thought of Moslems, it is no wonder that general history was regarded with little favour as a subject for study. Everything—science, religion, and history—was brought down to the level and standard of the teaching of the Koran and the life of the Prophet. While caliphs ruled in a simple and patriarchal way in Arabia, literature was denounced as a thing of peril. But a hundred years later, when Haroun al-Raschid the Caliph [1] ruled in pomp and magnificence at Baghdad, there came the impulse for a wider intellectual refinement. The Caliph surrounded himself with men of learning, an educational system was established, and the head of his schools was a Christian ! Baghdad became the resort of poets, philosophers, historians, and mathematicians.

The caliphs of Damascus, Baghdad, and Cairo, influenced by their non-Moslem teachers, sought to advance learning, whether Islamic or not, to the utmost of their power. A study of Islam, however, shows that these men were not drawing their inspiration from their religious beliefs. Their impulse was derived from sources mainly outside Mohammedanism.

Since the domination of the Moslem world by Turkey, Islamic leaders have lost their love of literature outside Islam, and the last four hundred years have been marked, in Moslem lands, by a fierce fanaticism for everything Islamic and an intolerance towards other creeds and ideas.

The Growing Power of the Press

With the invention of printing there came a new force to Islam, and the Press has become the means of uniting, in thought at least, Moslems all over the world. Islam has stood before the world as a unity.

[1] See p. 19.

It has faced Christendom with a united front, and the Press determines the common thought between Moslems of India and Egypt, Arabia and Turkey, China and the Malay States. Islamic movements have thus become of international importance. When Italy attacked Turkey in Tripoli, Moslems of India felt the shock, and the struggle of the Senoussi (the Mohammedan community of North Africa) was watched by the Moslem world as the fight of the faithful against the infidel. Prior to the War the leaders of thought and life in the Moslem world were the heads of the Faith, the sheikhs of the Azhar University in Cairo, and the Moulvies (Moslem teachers) of India. These stood for a triumphant faith, strongly entrenched, and ever reaching out to world conquest.

Let us now look at some of the changes that are taking place, all making for the shifting of the emphasis once more from purely Islamic ideals to a wider outlook. The first fact that stands out, and it is verified by reports from the whole Moslem world, is that Moslems are learning to read. Arabia herself, unstirred for centuries by movements from without, has caught the fever. Mecca and Medina have a number of bookshops supplied from Cairo, Damascus, and Constantinople. The new desire for education is common to all Moslem lands. Schools are crowded everywhere, and the ambition of the young Arab to-day is to be able to read. Baghdad, once the seat of learning, is again turning to books. The Baghdad government bookshop during 1920 sold books to the value of Rs. 600, and two years later was able to report sales of Rs. 16,000 worth of books.

Technical books on irrigation, engineering, etc., are in demand, and Dickens's novels are frequently sold. What would Haroun al-Raschid say to Pickwick on the Euphrates ? Eighteen sets of the *Encyclopædia Britannica* have been sold in the last two years to Arab customers ! Baghdad boasts a dozen papers and magazines. Education is advancing along many lines, and we now read of Arabs with wireless sets listening-in to messages from the West.

Syria and Palestine, under Turkish misrule, never had an adequate system of education. Now, under the mandatory powers of France and Great Britain, illiteracy is rapidly vanishing, and schools of a sort are open in almost every village. Modern journalism has come to the fore. Daily newspapers, magazines, and scientific literature are increasing rapidly, and by no means all this Moslem output of literature is hostile to Christianity.

In 1913 the Hamburg Kolonial Institut purchased a collection of newspapers in Arabic only. They were mostly daily papers, and the total number in the collection reached six hundred and ninety-four. In the same year Professor E. G. Browne told the Persia Society that his collection of newspapers in Persian reached between three hundred and fifty and three hundred and sixty titles. Since then many have undoubtedly disappeared, but others have taken their place, and to-day the aspirations of the East are being poured into hundreds of papers and magazines. Here are the titles of some of the articles from Persian papers : Brotherhood—Independence— Union—Culture—Reform — Humanity — Civilization.

F

The Chief of the Kashgais, lord of thirty thousand black tents on the Persian hills, subscribes to the London *Times* and has Reuter's telegrams translated to him by his son's tutor.

In Persia in 1909 an article in a Tabriz paper on the "Emancipation of Women" drew an angry mob round the author's house, threatening him with crucifixion, from which fate he was rescued by the authorities who clapped him in prison by way of saving his life. Contrast this with Persia to-day, where the busy journalism includes at least one women's paper edited by a Persian woman!

Any visitor to Cairo standing at a certain street corner about 4 p.m. will see a line of boys waiting outside the publishing offices of the evening papers. The doors are opened, the bundles handed out, and a minute later these lads are rushing through the streets, exactly as their brethren in London do, shouting the latest news, selling the evening editions, boarding trams, hustling passengers on railway platforms, and poking their papers through the taxicab windows. There are two hundred and seventeen printing-presses in Egypt to-day, large and small, and from them pours forth a voluminous literature. Novels good and bad are translated and circulated, and Cairo sees every year new books of scientific interest. The seventy-seven newspapers of the city exercise an amazing influence upon Egyptian national life. In every village, after the post comes in, one may see groups of people sitting round on the ground, while some local sheikh reads the daily news and expounds to the ignorant what is difficult to follow in classical

Arabic. Mohammed said, "The ink of the scholar is more sacred than the blood of the martyr," and Moslems are learning at last the meaning of this saying, and are giving a new impetus to reading and study.

Turkey in many respects resembles Cairo. Daily papers and periodicals are widely read. Literature in Turkey has given a new meaning to such words as "nation" and "fatherland," and Mustapha Kemal has, in the development of his policy, used the Press for the educating of the masses to his schemes and ideals. It is a remarkable fact that in Turkey the young women are the chief reading public, and devour novels with a zest that might even rival that of their sisters of the West.

In North Africa, when the President of the French Republic visited Morocco and Algeria, several of the native leaders in their speeches advocated that French education should be made compulsory for the natives. In 1922 the Financial Delegation made provision, extending over fifteen years, for the building of a thousand new schools for natives in French North Africa. Morocco, Algeria, and Tunis have between them about thirty Moslem newspapers in circulation. The startling fact emerges that North Africa, through its educational system, literature, and the influence of a governing Western power, is rapidly becoming Europeanized.

In Malaysia more and more people are learning at least to read and write. The British and Dutch Governments, by their large number of schools for Moslems, in which instruction is given in the language of the country, have created a demand for reading matter, and the villages are full of young people who can read. The Dutch have established thousands of loan libraries in connection with Government schools.

In India the Moslem community is not untouched. One mission high school reports that whereas thirty years ago not more than three per cent of the pupils were Moslems, the enrolment of to-day shows four or five times that number. Moslem literature is quite a considerable force in the land, and the country is flooded with political books, pamphlets and newspapers. Books by rationalistic European writers are translated by Moslem scholars, and these books find their way throughout the whole of India.

The old Arab idea of Islam, according to which all knowledge, science, and religion were found in the Koran, the Faith was exclusive, and no Moslem could see anything good outside the fold, is passing away. A new Islam is appearing, almost unrecognizable by the orthodox. Efforts are made to reconcile religion and science. The Moslem world, in its new desire for education and thirst for knowledge, is shifting its moorings. There is a revolt in many places against Moslem domination. The impact of Western thought on Islam has perhaps never been so strong as it is to-day, and there is a pathetic search going on for the best that the West can give.

The Need for Christian Literature

Into this world of Islam has come the missionary, and with him Christian literature. Raymond Lull was probably the first missionary to Moslems to understand the value of the written page. His efforts to rouse the Church of his day were fruitless, but he laid foundations for the study of Oriental languages, and what the Church failed to do he attempted, both by his pen and by his life. Henry Martyn gave his life in an effort to translate the Bible into Persian. Thus the first missionaries emphasized the power of the printed page. Missionaries to Moslems were faced not with a pagan tribe without a written language, but by Arab scholarship " with a world of books impossible to ignore." They set out to convert a people who were equally anxious to win the missionaries to the Faith of Islam.

And what was that Faith ? Imagine a young and ardent missionary preaching to a Moslem audience on St John iii. 16 : " God so loved the world that He gave His only begotten Son." "God": here surely was common ground, and yet the preacher soon learned that his conception of God was something widely different from a Moslem's idea of " Allah." " God so loved " : Does God love ? the Moslem asks, and well he may, for he believes that whatsoever comes to pass in the world, whether good or bad, proceeds entirely from the Divine Will, and has been for ever fixed and recorded on a preserved tablet by the pen of fate. " God misleads whom He will, and whom He will He guides," says the Koran (Sura, 14, verse 4). The missionary continues to explain God's universal love when a Moslem again interrupts with the angry exclamation, " I ask forgiveness of God for such blasphemy." No, there can be no love of God outside Islam, for all non-Moslems are destined from eternity to the fires of hell. In vain the preacher tries to explain, and says, " He gave His only begotten Son." Here a storm of protest follows. One exclaims, quoting from the Koran, " ' God neither begets nor is begotten.' How then can He have a son ? " The missionary appeals to the Scriptures, and the Moslems retort : they are corrupted ; the Koran has superseded them. He tries to lead his audience to Calvary, and yet another difficulty appears, and one in the meeting protests that Christ was not crucified : He did not die, but another upon whom God stamped the likeness of Jesus.

The audience continues to ask questions, and the missionary finds he is faced with people who deny the divinity of our Lord and exalt Mohammed above our Saviour.

Is it any wonder in such circumstances that controversy became inevitable, and that to meet Moslem objections to Christianity an entirely new literature had to be produced ? For example, it would be hopeless to try to use the same literature for a Hindu as for a Mohammedan. To the Moslem Christ is only a man, and Christians worship three gods. The Christ whom Moslems know is but a caricature. It is not what the Moslem does *not* know about Christ, but what he thinks he knows that puts him in a class by himself, and creates a special problem demanding special treatment in literature. How thoroughly the missionaries have done their work is seen by the fact that there is to-day a library of Christian books in some language or other which meet all the main lines of the Moslem's objection to Christianity. The great task before the missionary societies now is to make this missionary output available by translation and other means in all parts of the Moslem world.

Missionaries during the past fifty years have learned much, and probably some of the older controversial works should now be scrapped. Christians have come to understand the Moslem mind better, and through this experience have learned to approach the Moslem not as an antagonist, but rather in the spirit of love as one brother seeking to help another along life's way. " With such a spirit abroad we may look for all the ingenuity of love in finding ways by which Truth may reach a brother's life."

With the new literacy and outlook in Islam there have developed new lines of attack by Moslems on the Christian Faith. It would be quite a mistake to imagine that the Christian missionary is always the attacking and the Moslem the defending force. The very reverse is often the case. Aligarh (in India) and Woking (in England) stand for a new type of Moslem apologetic. " The character of our Lord is deliberately besmirched and the character of Mohammed is as deliberately glorified and painted in colours that would have amazed the Arab world of the seventh century. There is an attempt to make Mohammed the ethical ideal for mankind, and this has involved the painting of a new Mohammed in colours drawn from a Christian paint-box."

It will help us to understand how varied missionary literature must be if we consider the different types of people to be reached. Those educated along Western lines should be mentioned first. Here the missionary is faced with a body of young men, often rationalistic, whose Faith has now little hold upon them, and who in many cases are either avowed agnostics or atheists. These men are absorbing Western education without the guiding and restraining influences of religion. For the consumption of this class there is poured into a country like Egypt a mass of immoral literature in French and Arabic. In North Africa the schools turn out every year from seven to ten thousand pupils able to read French, and these are immediately exposed to the anti-religious influences in many French circles. Here is a problem facing the Christian Church, and one that demands the very best type of Christian missionary that the Church can give to it.

There is a wider class of people—those who are just able to read. They are little influenced by Western thought, and in the main are loyal Moslems. The majority of women readers come under this class. For these people a large assortment of illustrated books is needed. There are millions of uneducated village folk who can only understand a simple colloquial language. The Bible, as at present translated into Arabic, is above their heads and too classical in style, and missionaries are beginning the translation of the Gospels into a simpler language to meet this need.

The above classifications do not include the eighty millions of boys and girls in the Moslem world, and their need will be understood when we say that the proportion of readers among the children is higher than among the adults. The new situation has made clear that "the lads are learning to read by hundreds of thousands, and yet the provision for their awakening powers, as far as Christianity goes, is almost *nil*."

Newspaper Evangelism

As we have seen earlier in the chapter, the Eastern has become a newspaper-reading man. Here Christian evangelism finds one of its most fruitful openings. While the pulpit and the platform reach their hundreds and perhaps thousands, the newspaper simultaneously and rapidly throughout a much wider area touches hundreds of thousands. The War taught the world what could be done by the Press in moulding public opinion, and the missionary has not been slow in learning the lesson. Far-reaching schemes are on foot for the use of newspapers by missionaries. Many papers are willing to insert articles on the Christian Faith if paid for, and already a good deal of experimental work has been carried out. The Christian Literature Society for China has succeeded in getting a number of articles accepted for publication by Chinese newspapers. In India the experiment has scarcely been tried, but the missionaries feel that there is a great opportunity which if seized might prove even more fruitful than in China. Missionaries in Egypt, perhaps more than in any other Moslem land, have made great use of newspapers for Christian expression. Articles have appeared in a number of daily papers, and in some cases they have been inserted free of charge. In North Africa newspaper evangelism has been tried in the French Press, and although the aim primarily was to reach the Europeans it was found that Moslems also read the articles, and came to the missionaries afterwards to ask for literature.[1]

The Problem of Language

Although the language problem is a serious one, and Moslems are found in so many lands from China across Asia to North Africa, speaking the tongues of their own nationalities, yet Arabic, the language of the Koran and Heaven, prevails over a wide area. It has always been a fixed point in Moslem orthodox theology that the Koran is untranslatable, and translations have from time to time been forbidden; although with a new and liberal Islam in India there are bilingual copies of the Koran, and translations are being used in a number of countries. To the Moslem the study of Arabic is of supreme importance. The tribes under Moslem influence in Africa are laboriously taught bits of the Koran, while professors of Arabic are sent to Peking to teach the language to Chinese Moslems! The importance, therefore, of Christian literature in Arabic cannot be over-estimated, and the language is still spreading. It is possible for a missionary speaking in simple classical Arabic to make himself easily understood from Northern Syria throughout Palestine and Egypt and for fifteen hundred miles up the Nile. The cultural centre for Moslem orthodox thought is Cairo, the largest city in all Africa, and with the Azhar University centred there, Islamic influence radiates to the most remote

[1] See the recent (1923) survey, *Christian Literature in Moslem Lands*

parts of Africa and Asia. Here Christian literature for Moslems is being written, and in this unique situation the present problem is being faced.

The Task before the Church

In the Conference of Missionaries from all over the Moslem world, held in Jerusalem in April 1924, the Findings Committee on Literature reported as follows :

There is clear and universal testimony that the present situation in the Moslem world creates a need for literature as a dynamic and penetrating instrument of Christian educational evangelism altogether without parallel in range and urgency in the literary history of these peoples. Literacy is increasing rapidly in several of the areas. This fact is to-day developing an expanding demand for literature. The revolutionary fact, however, which has transformed the situation is the new mentality emerging from the upheaval of thought and feeling during and since the Great War. The shattering impact of the War itself, the rise of clamant nationalisms and race movements cutting across Pan-Islamic policy, the Bolshevik ferment, the Caliphate agitation, the increased government of Islamic peoples by European Powers, the critical debate on the civilization of Christendom, the eastward spread of European scepticism, the rebellion against traditionalism and external authority, the hunger for knowledge of new scientific thought and invention, the canvassing of the status of Oriental womanhood, and some strong reactionary movements, are all factors in producing a profound and widespread change that can be described soberly and with precision as epoch-making. The urgency of the need is quite as impressive as its range; for the present plasticity cannot be expected to continue indefinitely.

The unity of Islam has been mentioned in this chapter, and yet efforts to analyse what it is often baffle the student of Islamic literature. It is not linguistic, for Moslems speak a diversity of tongues (although one of the binding forces is the language—Arabic—of their sacred book). Nor is it a political unity, for in spite of Pan-Islamic efforts there is wide divergence in the political and national aspirations between, say, the Moslems of Turkey and of India. Nor is it merely the unity of a common ritual, through the use of the same rites, ablutions, pilgrimages, etc. These customs are bonds that mean much in the life of the Mohammedan religion, but behind Islam there does lie a greater and more impelling force.

The basic fact of the unity of Islam is a common spiritual attitude drawn from the spiritual content of the Koran and of the personal character of Mohammed. In many mosques in Egypt, Turkey, and other lands two words stand out in big bold characters on either side of the place of prayer — MOHAMMED . . . GOD. Surely here lies the strength of the religion : the character of God as conceived by the Prophet and as revealed in the Koran ; and the character of Mohammed as revealed in his daily life. These, more than anything, colour the thought of Islam, its political aspirations, its social life, its spiritual vision and appeal.

This unity, based upon a common worship of God and a passionate devotion to the Prophet, has knit

Islam into a brotherhood, and it demands of us an equally strong bond of fellowship founded not on the character of Allah as portrayed in Islam, but on the revelation of the God and Father of our Lord Jesus Christ.

Missionaries have long felt the need of unity in the output of literature. There has been an insistent demand for some agency or channel through which this unity may find expression and function in a sharing of their common literary task; and a call for a pooling of literary gifts and products between one field and another. Workers in all Moslem lands are calling upon the home Church for recruits, and their appeal is one to which we cannot close our ears. They ask for a central organization [1] to promote co-operation and to see that all have a chance of sharing in the creative power found in any part of the field. To neglect this plea is to admit failure by the Church where Islam has succeeded. It would involve, moreover, handing over to a large extent the enormous power of the printed page to Moslem propaganda at a time when the Church should be gathering strength for a great forward movement which would mean

[1] At the time of writing a central committee on literature for the whole Moslem world is being organized which is to serve to co-ordinate thinking and action in respect to the production and distribution of Christian literature. It is proposed that this committee shall function through a central bureau or office, probably in Cairo. Missionary Societies are being asked to lend their best men and women on the literary side of their work. There is every hope that this scheme will, in the near future, be launched. If it is carried out as at present planned it will enable as many fields as possible to share in the productive energy of any one field. It ought to mean the dawn of a new day for Moslem evangelization.

a new presentation of the Christian message to the Mohammedan world.

Such a forward movement involves unity of action by all missionary societies working among Moslems. God has been preparing the missionaries for this, for they are co-operating as never before. Native churches, pastors, catechists, and teachers are feeling the need of united and joint efforts in the face of so great a task. The field, too, is being prepared, as we have seen, in many new and wonderful ways, and while we thank God for His preparation of all the forces of His Kingdom in Moslem lands, can we see any corresponding response in our Churches at home? The issue lies largely in the hands of Great Britain and America. God is preparing in the desert the way of the Lord along which He may send His messengers before Him into every Moslem land whither He Himself would come. Dare the Church at home, in the face of this, refuse to respond?

Surely with such an opportunity, and faced as the Church is with an overwhelming responsibility, the words of Abraham Lincoln at Gettysburg are appropriate: "It is for us," he said, "rather to be dedicated here to the unfinished task remaining before us." The missionary, in the face of this unique situation, reminds one of the British gunners in 1915. They had guns, but the shells were so few that they were ineffective in stemming the tide of the enemy's advance. The present output of literature is wholly inadequate to meet the need that has arisen. The staff of workers is ridiculously small, and the funds at the disposal of the literature committees so scanty as to cripple any widespread efforts of evangelism. To meet this situation the conscience of the Church at home must be aroused until, by the united effort of all co-operating societies, the Church in the field will be able to present a strong, united, and effective front to the world of Islam.

CHAPTER VI

THE NEW WOMAN IN THE MOSLEM WORLD

IT is the month of September in the Delta of Egypt. The temperature stands between 90° and 100° in the shade. The road lies thick in dust after seven months without a drop of rain, and the cotton-picking season has begun. It is the early morning, and along the road there comes a crowd of laughing, chattering girls. They sound merry and happy as they make their way to the fields to pick cotton. They have been employed by a wealthy landowner at 10d. a day, and they begin work about seven in the morning and finish about six in the evening. Each child is clad in a long loose garment, something like a night-gown, and a piece of string is drawn tightly round the waist. The girls plunge into the fields, take up positions in a long line, and begin operations. They pluck the soft downy cotton as it hangs from the bursting pods and stuff it into their garments, which are left open at the top. Soon the slim and graceful girls begin to change in size. The cotton bulges out all round them, and is only kept from falling to the ground by the bit of string round their waist. They go on picking until they assume alarming proportions and appear to be nearly as broad as they are long. They then fall out of the line and step on to a big mat on the ground, untie the string, and shake themselves vigorously until all the cotton has fallen on the mat. The string is replaced and they again go back to the field and begin picking. This work is continued for ten or eleven hours, and then with native songs, and much fun and laughter, they make their way home.

Follow the long journey this cotton takes and you will see it unloaded at the Manchester Ship Canal Docks and transported on motor lorries to the mills. Again you see another crowd of girls, in the early morning too, making their way to a large spinning mill in a Lancashire town. They are differently clad, with shawls on their heads, and they are much older than their sisters in Egypt; but they are handling the same cotton picked in so primitive a way, although they are using the modern machinery of an up-to-date mill in their spinning. It is just here that Eastern and Western womanhood meet. The machinery of the mill makes one almost dizzy with its hum of life, progress, and trade. The fields of the East appeal to one with their picture of the young Moslem girls entering upon womanhood, and faced with all the problems that life for a woman in Islam means.

Let us shift the scene again. A group of business men are sitting in an office in Manchester working out an Empire cotton policy. They are talking, not in terms of thousands but millions of pounds. What is the result? Great tracts of uncultivated land are irrigated, and miles of cotton fields spring up in the Sudan, Uganda, and other parts of Central Africa.

G

The Mohammedan is stirred from his isolation. He awakes to the influences of an Empire cotton policy, yes, and to much more. Cotton means money, education, Western thought and life, and the effects are visible on whole countries.

We have seen the simple peasant girl of the East, the industrialized Lancashire lass, and the forces that are linking up both East and West, and consequently altering in many places the face of the earth. They will serve to illustrate the changes that are coming over the position of women in Moslem lands. To understand these movements we must retrace our steps to the days of Mohammed to find out what he taught in regard to women.

Women under Islamic Law

In a sense Mohammed sought to make himself the champion of women, of whom he spoke with kindness. He tried to improve their position, and there is no doubt that his teaching was in advance of the pre-Islamic conditions of Arab womanhood. " Treat your women well " he said in one of his sermons (see Koran, Sura 4). But it by no means follows that because Mohammed tried to improve the lot of women he gave laws that would suit any age or civilization, or any race outside Arabia. He retained polygamy, and gave forth what he claimed to be a divine and an infallible decree permitting Moslems to marry four wives. He made divorce so easy that by mere repetition of the formula " Thou art divorced " three times, a man could divorce his wife with or without cause, and marry again. This process could be repeated as frequently as a man wished. The only limit to it was his income, for money had to be paid for each new bride. In this Mohammed set an example to his followers, but when he reached the limit of four wives and wished to marry again, another divine decree was forthcoming allowing the Prophet (as the favoured of Heaven) to marry as many wives as he wished.

Mohammed, in his laws about women, probably thought he was introducing progressive legislation for their protection. His ignorance of the condition of things even in his own day in the more civilized parts of the world was profound, and behind his laws it must be admitted lay the thought that women were not to be trusted. They were inferior in intelligence and character to men and should be permanently under the guardianship of their menfolk. This is why in Islamic law a woman has all her life a male guardian—first her father, or if he is dead, a near relative, and after marriage her husband; and if widowed she is given back again to the guardianship of father or relative, who claims and exercises the right to marry her again to a man of his choice.

The interpreters of the Koran lost the kinder spirit of Mohammed in their endeavours after strict and rigid interpretations of their master's teaching, and they soon fixed the status of women, their inferiority to men, their loss of freedom, and their bondage. The leaders of Islam decided the fate of millions of their womenkind from their own standpoint of male superiority. The laws thus fixed are more rigid than any laws of the Medes and Persians, for they claim a divine authority, they rule out development, they lose sight of nationality. They are eternal, absolute and final laws that allow of no change whatever. Is it any wonder then that Moslem women to-day are seeking to break loose from the fetters of a bygone age ?

When Islam spread, Moslem men were allowed to marry Christian women who were permitted to remain Christian, but the law was inflexible in insisting that all children of such a marriage must be Moslem. On the other hand, the law was equally rigid in forbidding a Moslem woman to marry anyone of another faith. This one-sided law meant wholesale proseletyzing, as many thousands of Christian women were compelled to marry Moslems. This was the common practice in every conquered country, and where the women refused to marry they were divided among the conquerors and driven into the Moslem harems.[1]

It may be argued that this is all past history and does not hold good to-day, but the League of Nations has itself supplied the answer to this argument. The report of a Commission appointed by the League of Nations after the Turkish massacres of Asia Minor in 1920-22 says: " In the districts of Turkey that can be reached from Aleppo there are at least thirty thousand

[1] Harem or Hareem is a word used specially in Turkey, Egypt, and Syria for the female apartments of a Mohammedan household. In India the word Zenana is used for the same place. The Koran orders all respectable women to remain secluded at home, not to travel unveiled, nor to associate with men other than their husbands or male relatives forbidden in marriage. In India the women's apartments are shut off by a thick padded curtain called a *Pardah.*

women and children still living in Moslem houses, most of them longing for rescue."

In the Turkish deportation of Christians from Cilicia and other parts, the elder girls and young women were separated from their families and either abducted or sold to Moslems. Thousands of girls have been detained in harems, and children were sold by the Turks *since the war* for £1 gold, and they can still be purchased in Turkey at about the same rate.

In West Africa, with a mixture of pagan superstition and Moslem theology, women are degraded by age-long customs, both vicious and immoral. In Arabia a man has been known to exchange his wife for a rifle, and both parties have seemed satisfied with the bargain. In Persia temporary marriages are very common : the Shiah sect gives the custom the sanction of law and even permits the ministers of religion (Islamic) to be the chief promoters of it, many of them accumulating wealth by this base means. This custom of "muti," as it is called, is a serious blot on Islam.

The conclusion forced upon all unbiased students of Islam is that women are treated to-day throughout the Moslem world much as their female ancestors were treated in the time of the Prophet, but what was then progress is nowadays a backward movement.

A recent student, M. André Servier, writes :

The Mussulman woman thinks and behaves as did the ladies of Mohammed's harem. Isolated from the life beyond her threshold she remains in the barbarism of ancestral custom. Her present condition compared with that of the women of other religions is that of a slave, a magnificently got-up animal ; a beast of pleasure in the rich man's house, a beast of burden among the poor, she is nothing but a poor creature handed over to the good pleasure of the male.   Condemned to ignorance by the egoism of the man, she cannot even build in hope upon the future.   She is the eternal cloistered captive, the eternal slave.   Her barbarism and her ignorance have their weight upon the children she rears and to whom she transmits her opinions and prejudices.   Ignorant herself she creates others like her, a slave she gives her children slaves' souls, together with all the vices of a servile nature—dissimulation, lying, and deceit.[1]

If this were taken as a judgment on all Moslem women it would be far too sweeping.   In dealing with womanhood in Islam one should remember that the " harem lady " is only one class, the upper class, in the Islamic social scale, and that outside this group there is a much larger body of women to whom the word harem scarcely applies at all.   The peasant class do not live in harems ; their houses are generally merely mud-huts.   The women share the toil of the fields with the men.   Boys and girls mix freely in the fields and very few, if any, of the peasants wear the veil.   Polygamy is not very common among the poor, and the nearest approach to home life Islam ever gets is to be found in the houses of the simple-minded, hospitable and hard-working peasants.   The free open-air life in the fields saves many of these poor women from mental stagnation and slavish dependence upon the will of their menfolk, and they develop

[1] *Islam and the Psychology of the Mussulman*, p. 210.

a character peculiarly their own, an independence and resourcefulness that often make them the dominating factor in their own homes.

A sad tale could be written if only one side of the picture were seen, but it must be remembered that many of the worst superstitions and evils are not Islamic, but are customs handed down from days long before Mohammed's time. The responsibility of Islam for them lies in the fact that it has never been able to raise its people out of them, and that it too readily adopted the customs of the people it Islamized. The laws of Mohammed, for example, have been said to suit the black races, and Islam has often been spoken of as " a good thing for Africa." This theory has been tested now over a long period, and the conditions of black tribes in Africa under the Moslem faith contradict it. The fact that Moslem women themselves are looking for help to the social ideals of the West, rather than to the precepts of their Prophet, proves again the failure of Islam to raise its people to any level of freedom and civilization. On its social side Islam is a bankrupt force, and, at least where women are concerned, the only hope lies in the idealism and teaching of the New Testament.

We have seen, owing to the belief that all the laws of Mohammed are the laws of God, how impossible it is for Islam as a system to produce any progressive developments to meet the changing conditions of different ages. The problem facing the Moslem world to-day is whether, in spite of all the laws of the Koran, and the example and teaching of the Prophet, Moslem women can free themselves from the fetters of the past, and so change public opinion as to claim and win the wider freedom and liberty enjoyed by their sisters in the West.

The Dawn of a New Day

Islam nourishes within its bosom many disruptive forces, but we venture to think that the greatest force for the breaking up of Islam will be the women themselves. The factors that have helped to create a new situation in the Moslem world to-day have not left the women untouched. In most Islamic countries women's education has first been started by missionary enterprise, and in some countries the missionary societies are still leading the way in the education of girls. But Governments have had to yield to the insistent demands for schools for girls. The young educated men are no longer content to marry merely pretty dolls; they crave something better, and they insist on their prospective brides being educated. During the past twenty years female education has developed at a rapid rate, and literacy among women is correspondingly on the increase.

Modern ideas have filtered through from the men into the harems, and the women are taking as great an interest in politics as the men. The cinema is to be found all over the Moslem world, and the newspaper, with its political appeals for nationalism, independence, and liberty, has sent a thrill of new hope through harem life.

Changes rapid and startling are taking place. Moslem women now attend public gatherings, and mixed gatherings too. They throng the theatres and cinemas. They are to be seen in cafés and concert-rooms. They are forming clubs where lectures are given on literary and scientific subjects ; even mixed clubs have been opened in some Moslem countries. In many places there is much greater freedom in the use of the veil. Parents are refusing to marry their girls at the early ages of ten and eleven, and this is having a marked effect on education : girls are now frequently allowed to remain at school until the age of eighteen and sometimes even until twenty. This in turn is creating a new spirit of independence among girls, and many of them are now earning their own living as teachers, journalists, or clerks in shops, banks, and business offices.

The report of the Constantine Regional Conference, held in March 1924, says : " At this moment of un-precedented opportunity, not only is the Government favourable towards our work among native children, but its schools are preparing our way by breaking down prejudices and opening out now horizons."

In Egypt, when the country was in a ferment of national agitation, the better educated women took a leading part in propaganda work. They had political meetings among themselves, passed resolutions, and sent deputations to wait upon Lord Allenby, the High Commissioner, and upon the Prime Minister in Cairo.

The writer stood recently in the streets of Cairo watching a procession of Nationalists. Scores of motor-cars slowly passed along and an immense crowd surged round them. Every few minutes the procession was brought to a standstill, and on one of these occasions a car pulled up opposite me. In it were seated five ladies. They were shouting as loudly as the men for independence, and one of the ladies, making use of the opportunity offered by the stoppage in the procession, stood up and addressed the crowd pressing round the car. The throng was composed almost entirely of men, but this did not seem to disconcert her in the least, and in a torrent of words she urged the people to demand their liberty and freedom. I turned to a man standing near and asked, " Now what do you, a Moslem, think of that ? " He said, " Our women surprise us. We never thought they had it in them." I think my friend scarcely grasped the full significance of the awakening of women to their new position. He imagined that when the political agitations were over the women would quietly go back to the old ways. But would they ? Surely for them the word independence carries a fuller meaning than it does for the men.

The women who had done so much to help the national cause in the days of agitation and trouble could not return simply to the old life. They had entered upon a new path, they had tasted a larger liberty, and they determined to press for their rights. Fortunately for them the educated men were beginning to take a more liberal view of life and to acknowledge the wrongs of their womenkind. The work of emancipation became not only the concessions by the men to the women's demand for freedom, but also a question of legislation : for the laws in Islamic lands in regard to women were the seventh century laws of Mohammed and the Arabs.

Some time ago a large crowd of young men assembled in a Cairo theatre to see a play. The theme was the marriage law of Islam. The story described the young husbands sitting in cafés while their wives sat alone in the solitude of their harems. In the second act the wives are seen together in one of the harems discussing their fate, their lives and their miseries, and their longing that their husbands should share the home with them. They are comparing their position with that of the ladies of the West, and the scene closes as they decide to act for themselves and to compel their husbands to be companions and helpmates in the homes. The scene then shifts to a street in Cairo. Crowds of young men are sitting in a café when suddenly the wives swoop down. Veiled they had issued forth from their harems to hunt for their husbands and to invite them to come home to share the evening with them. The wives found their husbands, and in an impassioned appeal begged them to come home, and the dramatic finale came with the triumph of the ladies who arm-in-arm with their husbands led them back to a new comradeship and home. The play was a success, because it describes aptly the feelings of the people, the desire for a new life and for better home conditions.

We have travelled a long way since we read of the simple peasant girls picking cotton, and we shall naturally ask what relationship these modern movements have to the great mass of the people. The women who are interested in liberty and freedom are only a small percentage of the population. Many women are indifferent to efforts for their social improvement, and as only a few of the village women can read at all they are naturally unmoved by the agitation of their better-educated sisters. Those, however, who are leading the movement are not fighting their own battle only. They are seeking for the improvement of the position of women in all Moslem lands, and they are gaining increasing support from the men. Books are constantly being written by Moslems against the seclusion of women in harems. The attitude of Moslem girls themselves is that they do not want an imposed morality. " We do not want the veil," said a Moslem lady recently, " because it stands for the inferiority of women." One of the most encouraging signs in Egypt is the way the ladies of Cairo are seeking to help the poor and illiterate. A number of women's societies have sprung up lately ; one is " The Young Womanhood of Young Egypt," another is called " The Feminist Movement." Already these ladies have started schools where weaving and home economics are taught. Their plan, they state, is to raise the intellectual and social conditions of women that they may realize their social equality with men. They are seeking to reform debasing and superstitious customs and to introduce legislation for the protection of women in cases of marriage, polygamy, and divorce. They are carrying on propaganda in favour of hygiene and better home conditions.

While the movements are confined to the educated classes, yet their influence is touching Moslem life in many ways, and new ideas are finding their way into towns and villages that hitherto have scarcely altered for hundreds of years. I arrived at a town in the Delta of Egypt. A Moslem who met me said, " I am sorry we shall not be able to see you much to-day. We are all too busy." " Why ? " I asked. " We are all getting married," was the reply. A rumour had reached the place that a law forbidding polygamy was to be passed through the Egyptian Parliament, and they thought the best thing to do was to make sure of another wife before the law came into force. This will show the difficulty of the problem. The majority of the people are not yet educated up to these radical changes. The poor are illiterate, and it will be a long time before this new thought penetrates throughout a country like Egypt, although at last the women have found strong advocates among their own number. Their needs are being studied and the outlook is hopeful.

Women in Turkey

Turkish ladies made their voices heard in the councils of the nations, and " despite all differences of opinion among the Turks themselves regarding the status of Turkish women to-day, especially of the new type of feminist leaders and reformers that has developed under the republic, the advent of an era of feminine progress in Turkey is an irrefutable and significant fact," says Miss Ogilvie, a close student of Turkish affairs.[1]

Progress in women's emancipation prior to 1908 (the year of the Young Turk Revolution) was slow

[1] *The Current History Magazine*, August 1924.

nople to draw up new laws on marriage and to present them to the Angora Assembly. Their proposals are that the age of marriage for men shall be eighteen, and for women seventeen. Below this age marriage is to be forbidden unless the court gives special permission. Monogamy is to be the general rule, with the exception of special cases when the court will be allowed to sanction a man's marrying two wives. It is proposed to retain the old Moslem laws forbidding a Moslem woman to marry a non-Moslem man. Divorce is no longer to be simply at the whim of the husband, but laws are to be passed regulating and restricting it. The rights of wives are to be safeguarded, and the laws, it is presumed, are to be on modern Western lines.

Conditions in Africa

Conditions in different Moslem countries vary to an extraordinary degree, although there are problems common to all. In North Africa progress towards freedom is being made in the struggle for emancipation among women of the poorer classes. Before the war it was a rare thing to find any respectable woman seeking daily work, at any rate before she attained to grey hairs. Now it is quite a common thing to see women, and often young women too, earning their own living. Even working-class parents are anxious to see their girls educated, and are sending them to French day schools.

But it is among the middle-class people in North Africa that women's emancipation seems most likely to develop. The young men who have been in

France simply demand that their prospective brides shall be educated and able to take an intelligent interest in their life and work.

The Mohammedan Sudan, marked on its women's side by some of the most degrading and revolting customs anywhere found in the Moslem world, is developing. The Government Maternity School in Omdurman, established within the last three years, has changed antagonism and suspicion into grateful acceptance by the women of the relief from suffering which skilled treatment can give them, and has already put an end in many cases to the old barbarous customs connected with childbirth. There is an increasing demand for education for girls, the demand coming even more from the mothers than from the fathers. The Sudanese are beginning to feel that what has done so much for Western women may be worth trying for their own womenfolk also. Legislative measures are being demanded by Moslem religious leaders in the Northern Sudan for the prevention of the cruel customs connected with marriage, and other similar reforms are under consideration. The spread of education for girls is raising the status of women, and there are evident signs that the Moslem Sudanese are tending towards a higher level of civilization.

The appeal from the women of Moslem lands to their sisters in the West is insistent and urgent. There are to-day unlimited needs and opportunities for work among women—in many instances through their own societies—in attendance of maternity cases,

H

in child welfare centres, and in visits by nurses to homes. Publicity work is needed in educating public opinion on the evils of child marriage, divorce, etc. There is wide scope for rescue work: in some areas babies are bought and sold; divorced girls need sheltering and befriending, and only the sympathetic touch of Christian women can cope with their need. It is clear that until the Church pays more attention to the winning of the women, Moslem evangelization will never really succeed. To evangelize Moslems, women's work in all its forms must play an increasingly important part.

When the Prince of Wales opened the new North Road in 1924 he said, it "marks the completion of the task bequeathed to us more than 1600 years ago by the Romans. They were the pioneers who blazed the long trail known as Watling Street through dense woods and over steep hills." This chapter has described the opening of another road, the trail of which was blazed by Jesus Christ, when, through Gethsemane and Calvary, He gave a new value to human life. The chains of slaves were broken when the Christian conscience awoke to see in mere "niggers" brothers for whom Christ died. Through Christ have come also the new aspirations of the women of the East for a richer and fuller life. The trail was blazed by love and agony, and the road for the emancipation of millions of Moslem women is opened at last—but who will travel that road? We look some years ahead and we see passing along it the best and finest of our Western womanhood, on their way to a service of sacrificial love for their sisters who are seeking their co-operation. Words alone will not help them, for the road is thorny and difficult, but deeds that spring spontaneously from the impelling love of God. Across this road to-day a banner floats which reads, " By love serve one another."

CHAPTER VII

THE MOSLEM WORLD IN TRANSITION

The Orthodox Attitude to Non-Moslems

OLD Orthodox Islam has been kept alive by the fierce Wahabis of Arabia (the Puritans of Islam), plunder-loving Turks, scholarly sheikhs of Cairo, and Mahdists of the Sudan; but in every age there has been conflict within the House of Islam, the one party standing for Islam and the destruction of everything non-Moslem, and the other party with more open minds seeking to adapt their outlook on life to a wider range of thought and tolerance. The conflict has raged in different ages at Damascus, Baghdad, and in Egypt, and the problem that has ever confronted Moslem leaders of all parties has been the reconciling of the claims of Islam with modern thought and scientific discovery.

Has Islam then, as such, ever changed? It is true to say that Islam as a religious and political system has remained unchanged from the time it was codified after the death of Mohammed until to-day. One illustration may be given of this. The Holy War has been one of the Moslem's principal methods of extending Islam. The world is divided into two parts, Moslem and non-Moslem, the " House of Islam " and the " House of War." Mohammed's instructions were, " Complete my work, extend the

House of Islam to all parts"; in another place he says, "Fight the infidels until there be none left." The principle laid down is that war is the normal state of Islam. Orthodox interpreters give but one comment on this verse: "There can be no peace with the infidel." It is rightly claimed that when Moslem armies started out on their conquests they had for their use of the sword the example of their Prophet. When after the Battle of Badr a number of Arab captives were being put to death, to one of them who begged for mercy the Prophet said, "I thank the Lord that he has delighted my eyes with thy death," and when the dying man asked who would take care of his little children Mohammed replied, "the fires of hell." The pages of Islamic history are stained throughout by fanatical outbursts, massacres of Christians and others, and the forcible conversion of non-Moslems to Islam. In battle their cry has been, "Kill, kill in the name of the Prophet," and in victory their terms have been "Believe or perish," "Believe or become slaves." Has Islam changed? In Chios nearly a century ago the Turks slaughtered practically the whole population of the island. In the report of the Armenian massacres 1914–18, we are told that twenty-one Protestant preachers and one hundred and seventy Gregorian priests were, after enduring unspeakable tortures, murdered on their refusal to accept Islam. The report goes on to tell us that such figures express only the extent of our information and do not by a long way reach to the extent of the reality.[1] All of us will remember

[1] Zwemer, *The Law of Apostasy in Islam*, ch. iv.

the terrible stories that reached us of massacres of Greek Christians at the sacking of Smyrna in 1922.

Down to the nineteenth century the Christians of Egypt were subjected to a petty form of persecution, which was designed to show the brotherhood within the fold of Islam and the difficulty and trouble of remaining outside it. Christians were not allowed to build churches or monasteries, and this became so fixed a rule that long after the British occupation of the country, Copts in the villages often had the greatest difficulty in erecting a place of worship. But even then there were always Moslems better than their creed. When the Christians began to build a church in one village about fifteen years ago, the writer well remembers how the Moslems opposed the scheme. Each day building work was done, and each night it was demolished. This went on for some time until the Christians visited the chief of the village and asked for fair play. To the credit of a Moslem village leader be it said this man took an oath that the church should be built. He subscribed to its funds, and personally stood by while the masons worked. In the end when the church was finished he attended the opening service, and made a speech in which he said he was going to see that there was freedom for all. This one man's action affected the attitude of Moslems in the whole of his district, and when missionaries visited the village on preaching tours, the old Moslem leader entertained them, and they were always free to teach his people without fear of trouble.

Christians in Egypt were, prior to 1882, forbidden to ride horses. They were compelled to wear distinctive dress, and to move aside to allow the meanest Moslem to pass, and they were not permitted to ring church bells. The visitor to the Near East to-day is often surprised to find suspended outside a church a long beam of wood. It was the substitute for a bell in the old days. Beating on a block of wood does not give forth any sweet sound, so the Moslems ordained it for the Christians instead of the ringing of bells, which always seemed to them to strike the merry note of a joyous faith. This they could not allow because they believed Christianity to be a defeated and dying religion.

Islam, self-satisfied and proud, sought by every means in her power to complete the conquest of what her followers believed to be a triumphant and victorious creed. They made easy the pathway from Christianity to Islam, and every inducement was held out to the Christian to enter the fold. He was offered wealth, women, and ease, if he would but repeat the creed, " There is no god but God, and Mohammed is the Apostle of God." Once the convert was safe inside the door he frequently discovered he had been duped, and awoke to find himself within the meshes of a net from which there was no escape. If he wished to return to Christianity he was faced with the threat of death for apostasy, for Mohammed had said that " he who departs from Islam, becoming disobedient to God and His Apostle, let him be cut off, or crucified, or destroyed from the earth."

The Growth of Western Influence

The last fifteen years have seen one long battle for liberty and freedom of conscience in Moslem lands. As Western influence grew, Moslems slowly awoke out of their long slumber, and as the might of Europe spread eastwards the isolation of the Islamic world disappeared. Moslem life was drawn into the great stream of Western civilization and thought, and gradually changes came. At first a small cloud like a man's hand appeared, but the influence of the West penetrated far and deep into the tradition of the past until the small cloud grew into a blackened sky, the evident sign of a coming storm. The influences at work were non-Moslem, and the orthodox believers watched with growing apprehension the modernizing tendencies of a rising generation. Strenuous efforts were made to revive Islam. Anti-Christian and other literature poured from scores of printing presses. Dervish [1] orders redoubled their zeal. Pageants and processions were organized, and a great increase in the number of pilgrims to Mecca followed. Moslem teachers travelled far and wide exhorting the faithful, rebuking the careless, and defending the faith. European powers listened gravely to the warnings of Moslem leaders and adopted a sympathetic attitude towards Islam. Nothing, however, could check the storm, and in recent years it has struck with full blast

[1] The word Dervish or " Darwish " is Persian, and means a religious mendicant. Translated literally it is " one who goes from door to door." It is now used for those who lead a religious life. These people are banded together into " orders," corresponding to the Franciscan and other religious orders in the Church.

upon the faith. We must now try to describe the effects of the growth of Western influence upon Christian missionary enterprises.

Western mechanical inventions have left the Moslem world behind, and as a military power it has ceased to count. The domination of large areas of the Moslem world by European powers has relieved the harassing conditions of Christians and other non-Moslem peoples. It has been impossible, for example, for Moslems to apply the Law of Apostasy in lands under British and French control, and some measure of equality has been given to the hitherto persecuted non-Moslems.

Prior to the War, freedom of conscience was guaranteed throughout India by the British. In the Dutch Colonial Empire there is equal liberty. " Everyone," so runs the law, " shall have complete freedom to confess his religious beliefs," and Dr Zwemer reports after a recent visit to Malaysia that " there is complete freedom for the person of converts in the Dutch East Indies, and the Law of Apostasy has become a dead letter." Probably because of this freedom the missionaries in the Dutch East Indies have been able to build up a Church with about forty-five thousand converts from Islam. While before the War Moslem lands under Western control enjoyed a wide measure of freedom, yet this was not in any sense true of those countries controlled by Moslem powers. Turkey still maintained an attitude of hostility and violence towards any would-be Christians, and most converts had to flee the country.

Opening Doors for the Gospel

As a result of the War, Palestine, Syria, Mesopotamia, and parts of Africa, have become mandated
territories, and in all treaties drawn up by the
League of Nations there are clauses which provide for
missionary freedom and liberty of conscience for the
natives. Here is the clause in the Mesopotamia
(Iraq) treaty drawn up in 1923 :

No measure shall be taken in Iraq to obstruct or
interfere with missionary enterprise or to discriminate
against any missionary on the ground of his religious
belief or nationality provided that such enterprise is
not prejudicial to public order and good government.[1]

The new constitution for Egypt provides for
" absolute freedom of conscience."

The treaty of Lausanne between the Entente
Powers and Turkey, Article 38, reads :

The Turkish Government undertakes to assure full
and complete protection of life and liberty to all
inhabitants of Turkey without distinction of birth,
nationality, language, race, or religion. All inhabitants of Turkey shall be entitled to free exercise,
whether in public or private, of any creed, religion,
or belief.

These treaties make countries hitherto closed to
Christian teaching geographically accessible, but the
mere right to preach and teach in a country does not
necessarily mean that the country is open to the
Gospel. Mental accessibility is far more important
than any geographical openings, and our next question

---

[1] Quoted in *The Moslem World*, January 1924.

is, How far are Moslem *people* to-day open to the influence of the Gospel? It was estimated at the Jerusalem Conference held in April 1924 that roughly four-fifths of the people of the Moslem world are now " increasingly accessible to every method of missionary approach." Moslems are being converted in increasing numbers, and the problem facing the Church has now changed from the old one of inaccessibility to the new one of the training of adequate forces of workers and the right distribution of those forces.

How does this "accessibility" come about? Imagine an isolated village, say thirty years ago, hidden in a grove of palm trees. No roads run through it, the only means of access to it are narrow paths. Visitors are compelled either to walk or ride horses, donkeys, or camels. One day a boy proudly rides off on a donkey to take the train for the nearest town where there is a Government school. For the next eight years he absorbs the teaching of the West. At the end of the time he returns to look after his father's land, but his life at school has changed his outlook, and the village seems a backward place, the people he thinks stupid and ignorant, and he sets himself to reform his district. A road is opened, a motor-car bought, and a school built. Within a few years a number of youths can read. Newspapers find their way into the village. The people begin to take an interest in the outside world. A motor-bus is started and the journey to the town becomes cheap and easy, and so the movement goes on. Politics enter into the life of these simple peasants, and the young man finds he no longer has a docile tribe to rule but an independent and sometimes defiant people. A missionary visits the village and the Moslem leaders try to arouse the fanaticism of their followers, and are surprised when instead of driving out the Christian preacher the villagers demand a hearing for him and listen attentively to what he has to say. For twenty years or more these changes have been going on quietly, and in many Moslem countries to-day a new spirit is visible, a spirit of toleration and independence of thought and action.

Persia is an illustration of this. The old persecuting edicts have never been cancelled, and according to the laws of the land Persia is not open to the Gospel, but the people have gone ahead of their laws. Converts have boldly claimed a wider freedom than the laws allowed, and native churches of Moslem converts are being built up because the people are themselves accessible. There are over four hundred converts in Persia from Islam and they have all been baptized *openly* in the Church. Two of the native clergy are Moslem converts, and members of the native Church, inspired by the missionary ideal, are reaching out in a widespread evangelism for the conversion of their brother Moslems. The new tolerance in Persia is evidenced by the fact that two to four hundred Moslems attend a meeting in one town every week which is addressed by a Moslem convert to Christianity.

One missionary received an application from a Moslem town in Persia to open up work. He had to refuse it through lack of funds. The Moslems then enquired how much money was needed, and when they were told the sum, they collected the whole amount among themselves, paid the money into a bank, and posted the receipt to the missionary with a renewed appeal for a worker. Ninety-five per cent of the population of Persia is Moslem, and the law says " nothing shall be taught contrary to Islam," but here is an aggressive missionary work, a widespread evangelism, a native Church with pastors chosen from Moslem converts. But the Persian Church had its days of persecution, and it has an honoured roll of martyrs. The seed was sown amid discouragement and opposition : to-day God is giving the harvest.

In South Arabia thirty years ago when Dr Young went on his itinerating tours, an escort of Moslem soldiers was sent with him, and they always forbade anyone to listen to the preaching. Prejudice was so strong that preaching became almost impossible. To-day Dr Young tells how prejudice is broken down, how he is welcomed now by the tribes who previously refused to listen to him.

In a lecture given before the Central Asia Society in October 1924 by Lieutenant-Colonel H. Jacob, on the trade opportunities of South Arabia, a splendid tribute was paid to the Medical Mission at Aden. The speaker, in mentioning British assets in the Yemen, instanced the successes of the veteran missionary, Dr Young, and his associates of the Keith-Falconer Mission, and said that their work was the prime political asset of Great Britain. This is interesting as an example of the changed attitude of many British officials to Christian missions among Moslems. One thing is now clearly proved : missionaries, instead of arousing and increasing fanaticism, actually help towards a more tolerant outlook by Moslems. If our own officials have been slow to appreciate the work of mission schools and hospitals the Moslems themselves have quickly seen their value, and they are responding to-day by an increasing desire to know what it is that makes missionaries willing to give their lives for the service of Islamic lands.

In Syria where, up to 1924, any convert or even enquirer was in danger of arrest and of being condemned to death, there is a new and in many ways a unique situation. New roads have linked the towns and villages together and motors run to the most remote parts of the country. The old Turkish restrictions have been removed and the missionaries are free now to preach and teach. There is a new freedom of the press, and under the French mandate liberty of conscience is guaranteed. More remarkable still, though, is the new thirst for all kinds of Western knowledge. Secondary schools in Syria before the War had very few Moslem pupils, but to-day one-third to a half of the students are Moslem. With the overthrow of Turkey a new national self-consciousness has arisen, and people speak of liberty and independence in a new way. The old leaders of Islam have watched the trend of events closely, and in such towns as Damascus they have bitterly opposed missionary work, and in one instance petitioned the Government to turn the missionaries out of the country. It should be remembered that in all these lands, even where conditions are most favourable, there is always a large number of the old orthodox Moslems who view with equal distrust Christian activity and modern tendencies among the younger generation of Moslems.

Egypt is to-day entirely accessible to the Gospel in every direction, and it is possible to preach Christianity in every town and village. As mentioned earlier, the Nationalist Movement led to a strange alliance between Moslems and Christians in 1919, and the Cross and the Crescent were stitched on the one flag. Political aims were exalted above religious demands, and for a time the educated thought and talked nothing but politics. It is a strange coincidence that at this very time a party of missionaries travelled in a houseboat down the Nile preaching everywhere, and reported that they had had unlimited openings for the Gospel. They found the people willing to listen to the message. The old bigotry and fanaticism seemed to have disappeared and there was a spirit of enquiry among the Moslems wherever they went. This new situation has been verified from all parts of Egypt, and everywhere one hears of new openings and more enquirers. Perhaps in no other Moslem country is evangelistic work so widespread and thorough. It is possible now to distribute Bibles and Christian literature in the Azhar University itself. More Moslems are attending mission schools, and the missionaries feel, as Dr Mott put it at the Conference at Helwan in March 1924, that " We are on the threshold of something truly great."

In Eritrea half the population is Moslem. Formerly it was a Christian country, but it is estimated that in the last century two hundred thousand Christians Islamized. Thirty years ago no Moslem was allowed to attend a mission school. Now parents are eager to send their children to the missionaries, and two hundred baptisms of Moslems are reported.

In Abyssinia there are two to three million Moslems and four million Christians, members of the Coptic branch of the Eastern Church. A very remarkable movement has been going on in recent years among the Moslems and there are about seven thousand converts from Islam. The movement started through the teaching of a converted Moslem sheikh.

North Africa a century ago was a wild land without roads or means of transport. To-day it is covered with roads and railways and is everywhere geographically accessible. The Sahara has been traversed by motor parties and four railways penetrate into the desert. Politically the country is open too, and the missionaries are free to go ahead in almost all branches of work. There are over a million Europeans settled in North Africa and the impact of Western thought on the native population is having a marked effect. Half a million natives enlisted in the French army during the War, and to-day there are forty-five thousand North Africans living in and around Paris. Travel is easy, and many thousands of natives visit Europe. The people are losing the old fanatical spirit that moved them when they dragged Raymond Lull outside the town of Bujia and stoned him to death. A new tolerance is seen, and converts are baptized now without the haunting fear of death awaiting them when they appear in public.

The Methodist Episcopal Church is doing a remarkable work in North Africa, and the report of their missionaries for 1924 speaks of baptisms and converts, of progress and encouragement. One missionary says, " We are on the eve of deep and wide changes in Tunis—changes having their origin in a political movement and social ferment, which in turn are exerting a slow disintegrating effect upon the block of Islam." In four years the native Christian membership of this Church has increased from forty-seven to eighty, probationers from thirty to one hundred and sixty-eight. " Many things," says Dr Freize, " indicate a much more tolerant attitude of North African Moslems toward Christianity. One instance is the radical change in the view-point of the young men. Another instance is the willingness, and even eagerness, of parents to commit their children to our ' Homes.' Missionaries of all missions unite in testifying that the general attitude of Islam to Christianity has radically changed for the better."

In far-off Turkestan, we hear from the missionaries that " Moslems are coming in hundreds to hear the Gospel," and that enquirers are coming forward in increasing numbers.

One report from a Moslem area in India says, " All India is open to the Gospel. The reform movements initiated by the Aligarh Moslems are making for a wider liberty and a more tolerant policy. This new spirit has been noticeable even among the old orthodox

I

type of Moslems who are now much more accessible to the Gospel."

It may surprise some to learn that in Peking, China, there are thirty-eight mosques, and a school with two hundred and thirty pupils run by a Turkish Professor from the Azhar University in Cairo. In Nanking there is a theological college for Moslem students. The head of it spent a year in Mecca before taking up his duties in China. Thirty years ago a Chinese pilgrim to Mecca could scarcely be found in Peking or the neighbourhood. To-day there are some communities entirely composed of Moslem pilgrims. Every year many Chinese make the pilgrimage to the tomb of the Prophet in Mecca. What is the attitude of these Chinese Moslems to the Gospel to-day? There has in recent years been a revival of Islamic ideals among Chinese Moslems, and Turkey has taken an active interest in the Moslems of China; but there has also been a growing willingness on the part of these people to listen to the Gospel. Throughout the whole Empire they are accessible to the missionary, and in some respects are more disposed to be friendly than non-Moslem Chinese. The Chinese Moslem appears to have no objection to entering a Christian place of worship or to listening to the Gospel.

Perhaps the accessibility of Chinese Moslems to Christianity can be best illustrated by one missionary's testimony after years of preaching among them. " I can always," he says, " get access to their mosques, and in them I have perfect freedom to present Christianity. . . . The Moslems of Yunnan were never more accessible. We receive far more invitations to the mosques to discuss the Gospels than we can possibly accept." Aggressive Christian propaganda is going on. The doors are open everywhere, and all that is needed is a band of workers to help in the great task before the Church in China.

The Last Doors

Much has been said in this chapter about the open doors in Moslem lands, but what about the countries still fast closed to missionaries? Parts of Arabia and Afghanistan have been impossible spheres of missionary enterprise. In the areas surrounding Mecca and Medina in Arabia the missionary has been forbidden to enter. But the spread of the Gospel does not depend on the European missionary alone. The Bible, translated into Arabic, has found its way into the sacred places of the Prophet. Copies of the Scriptures have been sold in Mecca and Medina, and there is evidence to show that they have been eagerly studied. Moslem Arabs from Mecca travel up through Transjordania and into Palestine. Numbers of them have been treated by the missionary doctors at Amman and Salt, and they have carried back into the closed lands the message of a divine love, hitherto unknown to them.

In Afghanistan, where Islam has reigned supreme for centuries, and where Western influence has seemed to make little or no impression, a new day has dawned. Some of the leading officials are introducing wide and far-reaching reforms. Indian newspapers give us interesting accounts of the Amir of

Afghanistan's zeal for education. Schools have been opened in many places, and the problem of the nomadic tribes, who move about from place to place in search of pasture for their flocks, is being solved by travelling schools which are attached to the tribes and move with them. In Kabul there is a French High School with over three hundred *girl* students. There are now hospitals in the capital for women as well as men, and French, Italian, and German professors and doctors have been brought to Afghanistan to conduct the more important of these institutions. Public gardens have been laid out on European lines and a state band plays in the evenings! Can we estimate what this is going to mean in only a few years' time for Afghanistan and for the North-West Frontier of India? The wild tribes that have periodically poured into India, and that have in recent years perpetrated a succession of outrages, are at last coming under the educational and social influences of the West. If the experiences of other lands are any guide at all, this must mean the disappearance of fanaticism and the opening of this country to missionary enterprise.

The first sign of this is the fact that medical missionaries have at last been allowed to enter Afghanistan. The American missionaries at Meshed in North Persia have long wanted to enter the forbidden land, and for some time past they have been negotiating for this privilege with Afghan patients who came across the Frontier to their hospital. Efforts were made to get passports through the Afghan consul and the Central Government in Kabul, and on May 10, 1924, a little band of medical missionaries entered Afghanistan. Two busy weeks were spent in Herat. This town is situated on the extreme west of Afghanistan and is the pivot of the whole Central Asian question. It is a great trade centre, and caravan routes lead from it to all parts of Central Asia, Persia, and India, and here the missionaries began their work. " It would be hard," they write, " to imagine a more favourable or more interesting experience than we have had. The medical work has been nothing short of wonderful. The officials of the city and of the Province have shown us every kindness, and we have had opportunity to get some conception of the ' Young Afghan ' movement, its purpose, its successes, and its hopes." " When Christian countries," concludes the account of this interesting tour, " do their duty in helping this remote little kingdom as opportunity may be afforded, medically, educationally, and industrially, there will be a direct and honest enquiry into the ethical and religious belief of those who prove themselves to be true friends."

" Islam reformed is Islam no longer," said Lord Cromer, and the efforts of Turkey, Aligarh, and Woking, to reform the theology of the system of Islam are proving the truth of this statement. The old Islamic system is being left behind by the people, who are in many respects ahead of their faith and their Prophet in outlook, culture, and civilization. Fanaticism has become unpopular because the people see there is more in the Christian faith than they realized. The efforts of Woking and Aligarh to combine the

Islamic code with Christian morals and ethics is a great tribute to the living force of Christianity to-day. Turkish republicanism has proved to be the very negation of Mohammed's policy and aims. The thing that matters is not the system, the codes, or the law of Islam ; we have seen how Moslems can break away from these when they wish. The thing that counts is the people themselves. They are moving. Like an avalanche, slow at first, but gaining speed as it bears down a mountain-side, so Moslem people are moving towards something. They are seeking for an unknown goal. In many cases they are seekers after truth, after a new and fuller life, after liberty and freedom, both in thought and action. " Quo vadis ? " cries the missionary as he meets them. Whither goest thou ? Can the answer be supplied by the Christian Church ?

CHAPTER VIII

THE NEW OPPORTUNITY OF THE CHURCH

I was cycling along the desert on the eastern side of the Egyptian Delta, bordering on the land of Goshen, when I came upon a man pegging out a claim of land. He had bought, he explained, one thousand acres of desert at 2½d. an acre. It was cheap enough certainly, but it seemed a waste of money. The desert was hot, parched, and dry; not a blade of grass was to be seen. What a fool the man seemed, to be spending time and money on so profitless a soil. He must have seen my incredulous look for he said, " Come back in ten years' time and look at it then." The incident was forgotten until some ten years later I found myself back again near the same spot, and anxious to know how the desert patch had fared, I made my way towards the place. I came across a canal, at the end of which I found a pumping station that was pouring a vast quantity of water into the land. At first I thought I had made a mistake. I saw a pretty avenue of trees with a bungalow peeping through at the end of it. On either side of the avenue were vines growing, and I saw, to my amazement, great bunches of black luscious grapes hanging down. I walked on until I came to the bungalow, and there I met the same man.

" It did seem so hopeless at first," he said, " but now it is bringing me an income of £1000 a year."

Isaiah said, " The desert shall blossom as the rose," and many people imagine he was speaking in terms of a beautiful idea, whereas he was giving us a plain statement of fact. Is not this a picture of the Moslem world as a field of missionary work ? Henry Martyn and others laboured ; the soil seemed hard, and effort useless. Water poured on to a sandy desert is absorbed, and in an hour or two after the place looks as dry and hard as ever ; and as these early missionaries poured out the Water of Life no impression seemed to be made. People at home said : " What a waste ! Nothing will ever make that desert productive." They little knew that the hope of the missionary did not lie in human effort, but in the great dynamic of the Gospel, the divine power to regenerate the lives of men quickened by the Spirit of God.

The early days of missionary effort were so trying and difficult that churches and societies left the Moslems alone, and it was frequently asked, " Can a Moslem become a Christian ? " Still undaunted, the few stuck to their task. They watered the land, they ploughed, they sowed the seed, and they waited and prayed for God's day.

In the previous chapter we have seen some of the changes that are coming over Moslem lands, and they are remarkably like the vineyard. The grapes are ripe and waiting to be gathered, the effort has justified itself in an abundant harvest. The only difference is that whereas the farmer had his reapers ready, the Christian Church, after encouraging missionaries to go out to these lands and after praying for a harvest, is little prepared for it now it has come. The call to the Church is to face honestly the responsibility of answered prayer and to meet adequately the situation which is after all the creation of the Church itself.

Let us look at this call as both a challenge from militant Islam and as an appeal from the very soul of the Moslem enquirer.

Islam's Progress

Islam on its aggressive side has made great strides in the past hundred years. In India probably not less than six million Hindus, outcastes and others, have become Moslems, and progress of a similar kind has been made in China, Turkestan, and other countries. In Africa the Moslem menace, during the past fifty years, has been a serious factor in native life. The Eastern Churches of Abyssinia, Egypt, and Turkey have lost many thousands of their members to the faith of Mohammed. Islam, coming as it did after Christianity, claims to correct and complete our religion, and to-day it challenges Christianity for the conquest of the world. How then is this menace being met?

What Missions are Doing

While Western literature has disturbed and shaken the minds of Moslems, Christian missionary work has given them new ideals and hopes. One of the greatest assets of the Church to-day is its social and medical work. The mission hospital has been a living witness to the spirit of Christ. It has given to Moslems a practical example of the meaning of Christianity. It has set before the people a picture of the love of God, and has done more than anything else to open the hearts of men to the teaching of the Gospel. It has obtained a hearing for the missionaries where otherwise the doors would have been closed. The relief of human suffering has often proved to be the best of sermons, and the response of the patients has invariably been invitations to their homes and frequently the opening of hearts and minds to the message of the Cross.

The C.M.S. Mission Hospital in Old Cairo has grown in the past twenty-five years into one of the biggest medical mission institutions in the world. Its influence has spread five hundred miles up the Nile, and literally thousands of villages are influenced that otherwise might never hear the Gospel. The special wards for the Egyptian anæmia cases frequently take in over six hundred patients at a time, and over one hundred thousand of these sufferers, many of whom would otherwise have died, have returned to their homes absolutely cured.

A number of the staff—including one of the doctors—are Moslem converts, and classes for enquirers go on continuously. Prayers and an address are taken in every ward morning and evening, and lantern lectures are given several times a week for walking cases. A staff of catechists is employed, who visit the patients individually, and there are often over a thousand sick people sleeping in the hospital at one time. The names and addresses of all who come are written down, and visits are paid to many of their homes. Each year, in the winter, a travelling tent hospital is equipped, on the lines of an Army Field Hospital. The doctors go out in turn for a month at a time, and in this way follow up the more permanent work of the Old Cairo, and also carry out a piece of widespread evangelistic work. It is no exaggeration to speak of the broadcasting of the Gospel through this institution. Missionaries of every society in the land have spoken of its influence, and the itinerant missionary can always, in any village, find a welcome by the mere mention of the hospital.

In India the mass movements to Christianity are checking the spread of Islam. The rapidly growing native churches are a bulwark against which the preachers of Mohammed are failing to prevail. The spread of Islam in China is more easy as the Church has almost wholly neglected the Moslem problem in that country and there are not a dozen missionaries specially set apart for Moslem evangelization. In Africa twenty years ago Islam seemed to be sweeping all before it, and the great gaps between our mission stations were avenues through which the Moslem penetrated in his efforts to win the pagan tribes. To-day there is a chain of mission stations right across Africa from east to west, and wherever native churches have been established they have definitely checked the spread of Islam. In Uganda the early missionary work of Mackay and others was frequently frustrated and almost ruined by the activities of the Arabs. The struggle lasted for many years, but now the Christian faith is winning everywhere and Islamic aggression is rapidly coming to an end.

Eastern Churches seemed powerless before the strength of Islam and yet here, too, there are encouraging signs. The Gregorian Church of Persia is now running its own missionary society. In Smyrna Christian students of the Greek Church were recently imprisoned. They were driven from their schools and homes, scattered and persecuted, yet they had so learned Christ that they prayed for their persecutors, the Turks, and boldly preached Christ unto them. A young Armenian came to the writer in Egypt. He told a terrible story of how his family had been massacred by the Turks, and ended with an account of his conversion. He said, " After my conversion I could not love the Turks. The Moslems were responsible for all my misery and trouble and I hated them. Then I came to see that I could not be a Christian and harbour hatred in my heart, so I prayed that God would take away all hatred, and I promised if He would deliver me and give me His love for my enemies I would dedicate my life to Moslem evangelization." The struggle in his soul was intense, but in the end the love of God won the day, and the young man had come to tell me of his victory and to offer his services as catechist or evangelist to Moslems. This was some years ago, and ever since his keenness on Moslem work has been the most outstanding feature in his character.

The Moslem menace to these Eastern Churches is being met by a new spirit of love, and God is preparing many of the young men of the old Orthodox Church for this service among Moslems. Whether it be in Africa, Asia, or the Near East, we see at work the Church's one and only asset—the Spirit of God. He is working, and because of the Spirit of Pentecost the Moslem menace is being held in check. But is God so working simply to check the spread of Islam? Surely not. He is preparing men everywhere for *a great advance*, for the triumph of the Cross over the Crescent.

The Spiritual Need of the Moslem World

We have spoken of political aspirations, educational demands, and social efforts among Moslems, but these things lie very much on the surface. They are outward and visible signs of an inward and spiritual need. The fact is that Moslems to-day are hungry for something they cannot define, and their need goes much deeper than patriotism, and educational or social reforms. Many of them feel a deep need of God. A Moslem sheikh lay dying, and as he prayed he said, "O God, if Thou art just I am lost, but if merciful I may be saved." In the face of death his inner life was revealed and he felt his need of help. I stood some years ago beside the bed of a dying Moslem boy. His mother was near me. Earlier in the day a Koran reader had chanted the sacred book in the house, but in her hour of need the poor woman did not stop to consider whether she should use this or that form of prayer. Her need found expression in a passionate appeal to God for the boy.

Much has been written of the formalism of Islam as a religion, and people are apt to imagine that the Moslem has no spiritual experiences. A dervish, after one of the long chants in remembrance of God, was asked by a missionary what he got out of it. The man replied, "For hours we have been saying over together the one word God, and we have shut out the world and all thoughts of business, and our whole beings have been absorbed in the contemplation of God. Now," he added, "will you go home and sit for half an hour and say over to yourself the one word Jesus. If you will do this you will understand why we spend long periods in chanting the name of God." The missionary did it, and he understood afterwards a little of the soul-quest for God that lies behind much of the Moslem ceremonies and prayers. The dervish orders have their own liturgies, they hold prayer meetings and special missions. Their leaders act as pastors and visit their flocks and they claim to have a definite spiritual experience.

Orthodox Islam may be formal, but the Moslem soul is responsive, and if the outward crust can be pierced one generally finds underneath longings and hopes that can only be met through the message of the Cross. The outward crust is formed of self-satisfaction, a pride of race and religion, and a sense of superiority over non-Moslem races. This has in the past proved the greatest barrier possible to the progress of the Gospel. But look at the conditions to-day. The self-satisfaction is giving place to a profound uneasiness, and as new thought penetrates Islam, so the people feel that the things they have looked upon as unshakable are crumbling beneath their feet. The pride of centuries has been humbled by the disasters of the Great War, and the Caliphate question in Turkey has shown that one powerful Moslem nation at least has come to see that the boasted superiority of Islam is really inferior to the knowledge and civilization of the West. The missionary to-day finds the Moslem deeply conscious of his need and, therefore, open to listen to the message he brings. While a strict orthodoxy dominated the mind of the Moslem, little progress was made, but when the soul of the man is laid bare, when his need is uppermost in his mind, then comes the opportunity of showing him how his deepest aspirations are met in and through Jesus Christ.

We see, therefore, a whole series of events all converging towards one end. As those who believe in a divine government of the world we know God has a plan. Do we here get a glimpse of it? Had the Church not carried its message during the past hundred years into Asia and Africa we might have had a great Moslem power, political as well as religious, throughout Africa. Millions more of the outcastes of India would have embraced Islam, and ultimately the menace of a strong Moslem power might have threatened Christian Europe. We see God's plan, in averting this disaster, working itself out through the new life of the Church. But His plan carries us much further. All this has been a preparation for greater things to come. We have followed the events that are shaking the Moslem world, and here we see a further stage in the plan—the new attitude of many Moslems to the Christian Faith. Islam facing westwards may mean new political, educational, and social changes, but what will it mean for the Kingdom of God when Islam faces Christwards ?

We have studied a world preparation for the coming of the Kingdom of God. We have seen a world-need of redemption. We have watched the struggle through the last generation between militant Islam and the forces of Christianity, and we see a greater struggle going on now between the rationalism of the West and the faith of the Gospel. For what ? For the soul of the Moslem. We have watched the growing interest in Christian things on the part of the Moslem and we see the world of Islam to-day in a plastic state. This will not continue for long —the mind of the Moslem must ultimately set into some mould again. A Persian missionary said recently, " I have worked in Persia for forty years and I have never seen such an opportunity as now for preaching the Gospel." And this testimony is being echoed by missionaries from all parts of the Moslem world. This is indeed the great opportunity of the Church ; the opportunity to roll away the reproach laid upon the Church by Islam, and the opportunity of winning by love a people who have for centuries persecuted and crushed the Christian Faith in their lands.

A Neglected Task

The Moslem world has been neglected as no other field by the missionary forces. Mission Boards have looked upon Moslem fields as hard, unprofitable ground. They have sent their agents across them

OLD CAIRO MISSION HOSPITAL

Egyptian anæmia patients undergoing open-air treatment. "The itinerant missionary can always find a welcome by the mere mention of this hospital" (p. 139).

and beyond them, and the great block of Islam from Central Asia to North Africa has been neglected and in many cases untouched. When missionaries have sought to specialize on Moslem work they have frequently been called away to superintend districts, run schools, and do general missionary work, where Moslem evangelism has been impossible. At least one hundred million Moslem women and girls are outside the range of existing missionary effort. Of five thousand missionaries in India a tiny handful are related to the Moslem population, which is more than a fifth of that of all India. Other large areas are absolutely without any missionary. Here is the testimony of a missionary in China with a Moslem population of eight to ten millions :

The accessible Moslem population of China is two or three times that of Mongolia, is fully equal to that of Tibet, and probably not less than that of Manchuria. It may, therefore, be said that within China there is a special people, equal in number to the population of any of China's dependencies, for whom practically nothing is being done, and whose presence hitherto has been almost ignored.[1]

Recently the chief missionary societies in Great Britain were asked to supply information as to what they were doing among Moslem peoples in the fields in which they work, and here are some of their replies :

One secretary writes, " I am afraid we do practically no work among Moslems." Another writes, " I am sorry to say our Society is doing practically no work among Mohammedans." Another Society supplied in-

[1] Marshall Broomhall, *Islam in China*, p. 217.

K

formation of some work carried on many years ago and since sadly reduced. Another secretary writes, " I may say that my committee does not carry on any distinctive work among that people [Moslems]." The replies received were almost uniformly discouraging, and point to the fact that the Church has never seriously faced the problem at all.

Whatever reasons there may have been in the past for the neglect of Moslems by the Christian Church, surely these reasons do not hold good to-day. Was it inaccessibility ? The greater part of the Moslem world is open to-day. Was it the unfruitfulness of the soil and the lack of response from Moslems ? To-day the people are asking for teaching, converts are increasing, a harvest is coming, and God is calling to the Church, by many signs and in wonderful ways, to rise to its new and great opportunity.

The Islamic Review, the organ of the New Islam Movement, which in England has its headquarters at Woking, is advocating the acceptance of Mohammed as the ideal of the human race and his teaching as the standard of life for all nations. Christianity is attacked on the ground of its failure, and Christians are taunted with having lost the essential message of their Master. From another angle, too, our Faith is challenged. To the conservative Moslems the Cross is still a stumbling-block, and they refuse to admit the truth of Christ's death, primarily because the Koran says " Christ did not die," but also because they fail to see the message of Calvary interpreted in the lives of Christians they meet. The hindrance to the spread of the Gospel among Moslems lies more in the character of those who profess our Faith than in difficulties in our creed.

Thus there comes to us this challenge and call. Have we so lost our faith in Christ as to doubt His saving power for Moslems? Islam gives a challenge, but God gives the call, " Speak unto the children of Israel that they go forward."

Let us pick up again the thread of the story with which this chapter opened. The farmer had succeeded. He was growing his grapes and his income was increasing year by year. And then came the War. He was the subject of an enemy country. He had to leave his land. In 1918 I visited the spot again. There was a big crop of rank weeds, the vines were dying or dead, the pumping station was not working, and the land was again taking on a desert-like appearance. And here one saw a vivid picture of the mission station where recruits are withheld and the work is not backed up. The thin line of missionaries to Moslems is stretched to breaking-point. Some areas have, like the vineyard, been abandoned, and in others the labourers are far too few for the great task committed to them.

I visited, not long ago, a mission station where fifteen years ago European missionaries had laboured. They had preached throughout the district and a small native church had been established. But the lack of funds and workers had meant the withdrawal of the whole European staff, and it was pathetic to see an old catechist, after about forty years of service, all alone, struggling to keep his little flock together.

Members of an Eastern Church were again going over to Islam, and Christianity seemed to count for very little in the place. The villages of the district were unevangelized, and the Moslems saw Christianity as rather a weak and decrepit thing. Here certainly the sand was re-appearing, the fruitful soil was reverting to its primitive desert, and the Christian message was powerless to meet the situation because no workers had been sent there for years.

A Call for Unity

It is evident that not only are new forces and new workers needed, but those who know the missionary situation best are agreed that the day has come for the formation of a united mission policy in Moslem lands. The situation demands nothing less than a united front composed of *all* the Christian forces at work in these fields.   Dare we allow our church divisions to hinder the progress of God's Kingdom in these critical days ?   Are our party watchwords to drown the very voice of Christ in Moslem lands ?

While the leaders of the churches at home have been learnedly discussing plans for reunion, in the mission field the workers have been giving practical demonstrations of a new and spiritual unity, called into being under the sense of an overwhelming responsibility and in the face of a great task, and made real and effective by one common objective.

In most mission areas now there is an inter-mission Conference which draws together for united effort Anglicans, Quakers, Wesleyans, Baptists, Presbyterians, and others.   The neglected or unreached areas are studied, and it is becoming a recognized principle that where one society or church cannot do the work another should be invited to take it up. This has led to several joint and co-operative efforts, especially in literature and in educational institutions. In Jerusalem there are two colleges run jointly by three different Missions, the Girls' High School and the English College. The staffs of these institutions are drawn from the co-operating societies and the pupils are a mixture of Moslems, Jews, and Christians. Jerusalem has been the centre, since the War, of racial discord and the clash of Jewish and Arab interests, and there are few places in the Holy City where all three religions meet freely and on equal terms. In these two colleges they do. Jew, Arab, and Christian in the one college learn to play the game on the football field, and their esprit de corps gives a new outlook to the students upon the national problems of the day. Here we have members of three religions all studying daily the teaching of Jesus Christ. A new type of manhood and womanhood is developed which is making for the enrichment of social life, and Christ is presented to every pupil as Lord and Saviour, thus introducing a new spiritual note into the divisive influences of the city and making at last for " the peace of Jerusalem."

.   .   .   .   .   .

Here is our task. The issues at stake stand out very clearly, and as we review this story of God-given openings we ask whether this is to be yet another of the lost opportunities of the Church.

To sum up, the Moslem world to-day is in revolution because it is at last in vital contact with Western thought and life. This upheaval is a vast effort on the part of Moslems to keep abreast of modern civilization. Islam is on the verge of a new era. It is slowly detaching itself from the bondages of old traditions. The "unchanging" East is altering from day to day, and East and West are meeting on the common ground of the modern demands upon life. Orthodox Moslems are alarmed and horrified at the decay of religious beliefs, customs, and manners. The old fatalistic outlook is being replaced by an almost Ruskin-like creed of the sanctity of work. Moslems are no longer absorbed in an all-sufficient Koran, but are studying politics and literature, and as one of them recently said : " We are looking at our creeds now with a scientific eye." The old pride of Islam the invincible received a great blow in the world war, and Moslems to-day are thinking, not in terms of past conquests, but of future progress dependent upon their material and intellectual developments.

The emancipation of women was looked upon until recently as a crime against God and society, and yet, as we have seen, so rapid are the changes, that the restrictions upon women laid down by Islamic law are no longer tolerated. The equality of the sexes is advocated by Moslems through every type of printed literature, and men of the East now look with admiration, favour, and encouragement upon the efforts of their womenfolk to take an active part in political and social movements. This all spells a new attitude to life, an attitude born of a desire for the best the world has to offer. It is the awakening of a dormant soul after an age-long sleep. The soul of a great people is aroused, and for its possession there contends the anarchy of Russia, the materialism of the West, and the life-giving message of Christianity. The problem with which the Church is faced lies deep in the failures of the past. And the solution lies deeper in the infinite resources of God, upon which we can draw as we seek to face our task anew.

If we look simply at facts as they are, we are staggered at the magnitude of the unfinished task before the Church. In humble repentance let us confess our failure, and in living faith let us seek for a new spiritual quickening in our home churches. We need something like a mass movement in our own land, a return nationally to the simple faith of the Gospel with all its implications for social service and regeneration. Thus it was in the days of St Francis, of Wesley, of Whitfield, of Moody and Sankey and others. The Church through every revival of the past has received new life and power, and the conscience of the nation has been quickened to face great international problems, such as slavery, in the spirit of true righteousness. The people of our land to-day are conscious of a spiritual hunger which worldly things do not satisfy, and deep below the surface of education there is the desire for spiritual peace and rest and faith. The years since the War have, in many ways, been spiritually barren, but we are entering on an era of new hope and new faith, and there is a stirring in the depths that must mean new spiritual energy. God, who is preparing the hearts of men in India, Africa, and other parts of the world, is preparing too our home Church. The outlook of the world is fraught with menace and hope. Menace and disaster if we fail, but victorious hope if we unitedly dedicate our all to the great task before us.

The writer was invited some years ago to preach in a Coptic Church at the Great Easter Festival. The service began on Saturday night about 7 o'clock and it lasted until midnight. After the sermon and towards the conclusion of the service the priest entered the Sanctuary, the door was shut, and the young men of the congregation gathered round the west side of the door and sang the 24th Psalm. Halfway through one man knocked with his hand on the Sanctuary door and said, " Hath Christ risen ? " There was no reply, and he knocked again and asked, " Hath Christ risen ? " Still there was no reply. A third time he knocked, and the priest from within the Sanctuary answered, " He is risen indeed." Whereupon the man struck the door and sent it flying open and all the young men together cried, " Then let the King of Glory come in." A flood of light poured forth from the Sanctuary, the priest, accompanied by his acolytes, proceeded from the Sanctuary into the church, and as they appeared the whole congregation rose and everyone said to his neighbour, " Christ is risen," and all responded, " He is risen indeed." The church rang with the message. The galleries took it up and people standing outside in the street echoed it. Everyone called forth what has ever been the living message of the Christian Church, " Christ is risen—He is risen indeed." May we, too, take up the refrain, and in the spirit of our Risen Master go forth and go forward until the Cross triumphs over the Crescent, and Christ shall in all these Moslem lands have the pre-eminence.

THE MOSLEM POPULATION
OF THE WORLD

ACCORDING to the most recent census of the Moslem world,[1] the present Moslem population numbers 234,814,989, of whom 105,723,000 are under British rule or protection. The following list shows the main countries in which Moslem populations are found :—

UNDER MOSLEM RULE

Africa—

Egypt	11,658,000

Asia—

Persia	9,350,000
Turkey	8,321,000
Afghanistan	6,380,000
Arabia	3,400,000

UNDER CHRISTIAN RULE OR PROTECTION

Africa—

Nigeria	(British)	10,833,000
Morocco	(French and Spanish)	5,818,000
Congo	(French and Belgian)	7,464,000
Algeria	(French)	4,979,000
Sudan	(French and Anglo-Egyptian)	3,344,000
Tanganyika	(British)	1,276,000

Asia—

India	(Britain)	70,000,000
Dutch East Indies	(Holland)	36,000,000
Mesopotamia	(Britain)	2,640,000
Syria and Lebanon	(France)	3,000,000

In addition there are 9,136,000 Moslems in the Chinese Empire and 15,200,000 in Russia (in Europe and Asia).

[1] By S. M. Zwemer. See *Christian Literature in Moslem Lands* (1923), pp. 292-295.

SOME COMPARATIVE DATES

A.D.		A.D.	
570–632	Life of Mohammed	597 c.632	Landing of St Augustine in Kent Nestorian missionaries received by Chinese Emperor
749	Beginning of the break up of the Arab Empire	755	St Boniface, the "Apostle of Germany," martyred
786–809	Haroun al-Raschid, Caliph at Baghdad	768–814	Reign of Charlemagne in Europe
1071	Revival of Islam under the Turks	1066	Norman Conquest of England
1453	Capture of Constantinople by the Turks	1455	Wars of the Roses begin in England
1520	Turkish power under Suleiman the Magnificent extended from Baghdad to Hungary	1521	Luther at the Diet of Worms
1560–1605	Akbar the Great, Mogul Emperor of India	1558–1603	Elizabeth, Queen of England
1683	Last Turkish attack on Vienna defeated	1688	British Revolution—Flight of James II
1700–1800	Ottoman Empire in decay	1700–1800	European struggle for Overseas Empire
Early 19th century	Shrinkage of Turkish Empire—Turkey "the sick man of Europe"	Early 19th century	Industrial Revolution in Europe
End of 19th century	Rise of Pan-Islamic movement	End of 19th century	Partition of Africa

BOOKS FOR FURTHER READING

NOTE.—*Where E.H.P. (Edinburgh House Press) is given as the publisher, the books can be obtained from any Missionary Society. Nearly all of the books mentioned can be borrowed from Missionary libraries.*

RECENT BOOKS

Conferences of Christian Workers among Moslems, 1924. (International Missionary Council, New York. Obtainable from Edinburgh House, 2 Eaton Gate, S.W.1. 7/6.)

The Report of the recent Near East Conferences, culminating in the General Conference for the entire Moslem world at Jerusalem, 1924. This Report gives the present situation from the missionary standpoint, and should be read in conjunction with Stoddard's *New World of Islam*, mentioned below.

Christian Literature in Moslem Lands: A Study of the Activities of the Moslem and Christian Press in all Mohammedan Countries. (G. H. Doran Co., New York, 1923. Obtainable from Edinburgh House, 2 Eaton Gate, S.W.1. 10/6.)

A survey of the supply and demand of Christian literature for Moslems.

The New World of Islam. Lothrop Stoddard. (Chapman & Hall, 1921. 16/-.)

For advanced study—a careful account of the movements in the Islamic world which have led up to the present ferment.

The Law of Apostasy in Islam. S. M. Zwemer. (Marshall Bros., Ltd., 1924. 6/-.)

This is a clear and concise account of the law in Islam which forbids, under penalty of death, any Moslem to leave his faith.

Islam and the Psychology of the Mussulman. André Servier. (Chapman & Hall, 1924. 12/6.)

A brief history of Islam, defining the Mussulman policy of France. It traces the influence of Islam on world politics down to the present day, and ends on the note of "friendly support towards Turkey."

Spiritual and Political Revolutions in Islam. Felix Valyi. (Kegan Paul, 1925. 7/6.)

A new book written by a Moslem from the Moslem and Eastern point of view. It will be read with interest by serious students of Islam, though they will probably disagree with much in it.

The Crescent in North-west China. G. Findlay Andrew. (C.I.M. and Religious Tract Society, 1921. 3/6.)

An up-to-date and short account of the Moslems of China by a member of the China Inland Mission.

GENERAL BOOKS OF REFERENCE

Arabia, the Cradle of Islam. S. M. Zwemer. (Oliphant, 1900. 10/6.)

The Rebuke of Islam. W. H. T. Gairdner. (E.H.P., 1920. 1/6.)

The Story of Islam. T. R. W. Lunt. (E.H.P., 1909. 1/-.)

Aspects of Islam. D. B. Macdonald. (Macmillan, 1911. 8/-.)

Vital Forces of Christianity and Islam: Studies by Missionaries to Moslems, with an Introduction by S. M. Zwemer. (Milford, 1915. 3/6.)

The Christian Approach to Islam. J. L. Barton. (Boston, U.S.A., 1918.)

This book contains much valuable information on Islam, its spread, its strength and weakness. Modern movements down to 1915 are described.

The Contrast between Christianity and Mohammedanism. G. Dale. (U.M.C.A., 1908. 1/6.)

Jesus Christ and the World's Religions. W. Paton. (E.H.P., 1916. 1/-.)

Contains a useful chapter on the message of Christianity to Mohammedanism.

Modern Egypt. Earl Cromer. (Macmillan, 1908. 2/-.)

A long and detailed study of British influence in Egypt from 1880 to 1906.

Outlines of History. H. G. Wells. (George Newnes, 1924. Parts 13 and 14, 1/2 per part; or Vol. II, 22/6.)

The chapters on Islam and the Crusades are valuable for the broad pictures they give of the complicated history of this period.

The Koran. Translation by J. M. Rodwell. (J. M. Dent, "Everyman Series." 2/-.)

The Moslem World. A Quarterly Magazine. Edited by S. M. Zwemer. (Obtainable from Missionary Literature Supply, Church House, Westminster, S.W.)

Deals exclusively with the Moslem problem in all lands.

INDEX

158

BRITISH
ISLES

LONDON

GERMANY

EUROPE

RUSSIA

MOSCOW

PARIS

VIENNA

FRANCE

SPAIN

ITALY

ROME

BLACK SEA

CONSTANTINOPLE

MACE-
DONIA

TUR-
KEY

ANATOLIA

ANGORA

CASPIAN SEA

Volga

GIBRALTAR

SMYRNA

SYRIA

ALEPPO

IRAQ

MEDITERRANEAN SEA

TUNIS

MESOPOTAMIA

MOROCCO

ALGERIA

DAMASCUS

BAGHDAD

JERUSALEM

PE

TRIPOLI

CAIRO

SUEZ
CANAL

EGYPT

MEDINA

Tropic of Cancer

SAHARA

R. Nile

ARABIA

MECCA

Niger

SUDAN

ERITREA

ADEN

AFRICA

ABYSSINIA

Equator

UGANDA

SOUTH

Congo

ATLANTIC

MADAGASCAR

OCEAN

Zambezi

Tropic of Capricorn

CAPE OF
GOOD HOPE